JUMBLE®
Kingdom

A Royal Collection
of Puzzles

Jeff Knurek
and
David L. Hoyt

TRIUMPH
BOOKS

This book is available in quantity at special discounts
for your group or organization.

For further information, contact:

Triumph Books LLC
814 North Franklin Street
Chicago, Illinois 60610
Phone: (312) 337-0747
www.triumphbooks.com

Printed in U.S.A.

ISBN: 978-1-62937-079-8

Design by Sue Knopf

Contents

JUMBLE®
Kingdom

Classic Puzzles

JUMBLE®

Unscramble these four Jumbles, one letter to each square, to form four ordinary words.

CALVO

RSOYR

CTIERM

TLERIP

Print answer here

I remember this song from high school.

It's keeping us alive.

GETTING A CARDIO WORKOUT BY DANCING TO DISCO MADE THEM ---

Now arrange the circled letters to form the surprise answer, as suggested by the above cartoon.

JUMBLE®

Unscramble these four Jumbles, one letter to each square, to form four ordinary words.

REETX

SWKIH

AURROP

TILUGY

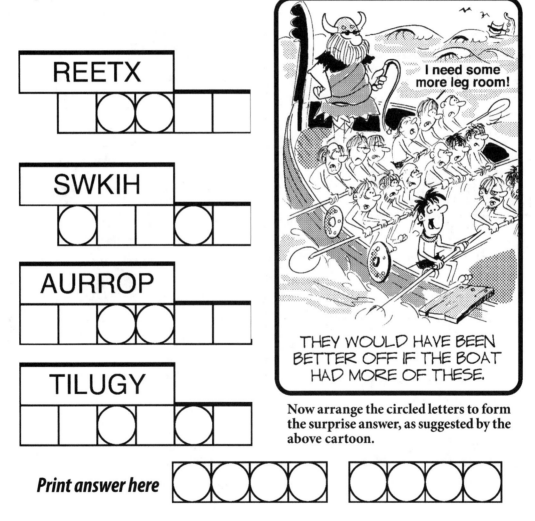

I need some more leg room!

THEY WOULD HAVE BEEN BETTER OFF IF THE BOAT HAD MORE OF THESE.

Now arrange the circled letters to form the surprise answer, as suggested by the above cartoon.

Print answer here

JUMBLE®

Unscramble these four Jumbles, one letter to each square, to form four ordinary words.

CINCY

HNITK

MEPEXT

SOFLIS

My collection will be safe out here. No one will be able to find me.

THE RETIRED HOCKEY PLAYER LIVED HERE.

Now arrange the circled letters to form the surprise answer, as suggested by the above cartoon.

Print answer here

JUMBLE®

Unscramble these four Jumbles, one letter to each square, to form four ordinary words.

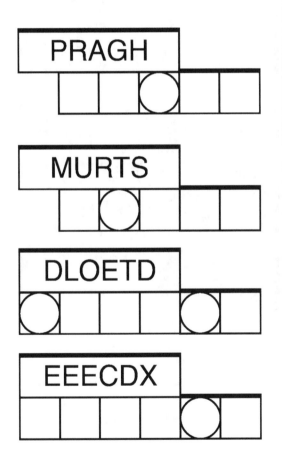

PRAGH

MURTS

DLOETD

EEECDX

Would you like an espresso?
I'm gonna need more than that!
ORDER HERE
ROAST & TOAST
Soup of the Day: French Onion

WHEN SHE ASKED HIM IF HE WANTED A SMALL AMOUNT OF COFFEE, HE SAID HE WANTED ———

Now arrange the circled letters to form the surprise answer, as suggested by the above cartoon.

Print answer here A

JUMBLE®

Unscramble these four Jumbles, one letter to each square, to form four ordinary words.

HYONE

KKISO

SOMLBY

FRACTY

Tonight YOU TOO! Live!

Happy St. Patty's Day! I'm Bobo and he's the Ledge.

YOU TOO!

Hey! That's not U2!

They don't sound anything like them.

WHAT THEY CALLED THE BAD IRISH TRIBUTE BAND.

Now arrange the circled letters to form the surprise answer, as suggested by the above cartoon.

Print answer here

JUMBLE®

Unscramble these four Jumbles, one letter to
each square, to form four ordinary words.

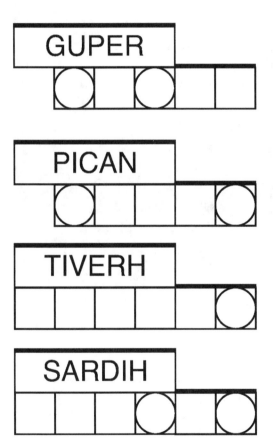

GUPER

PICAN

TIVERH

SARDIH

Wow!
It really feels
good to win
that pot.

AFTER WINNING
THE BIG HAND,
HE WAS THIS.

Now arrange the circled letters to form
the surprise answer, as suggested by the
above cartoon.

Print answer here

7

JUMBLE®

Unscramble these four Jumbles, one letter to each square, to form four ordinary words.

LRICE

EHANY

UETATM

GBREIG

I'm happy to tell you that you've been approved for your business loan.

HUDSON'S

HE WAS ABLE TO START HIS TRAFFIC SIGNAL BUSINESS AFTER HIS BANKER GAVE HIM THIS.

Now arrange the circled letters to form the surprise answer, as suggested by the above cartoon.

Print answer here THE

JUMBLE®

Unscramble these four Jumbles, one letter to
each square, to form four ordinary words.

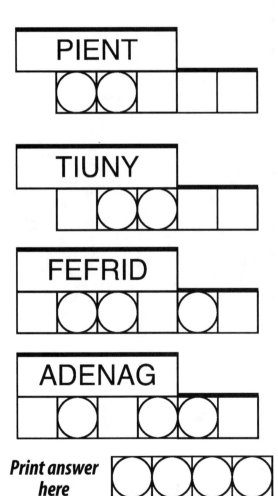

PIENT

TIUNY

FEFRID

ADENAG

I'm writing
you a
citation!
You'll pay
dearly
for this.

WHEN THE HEALTH
INSPECTOR FOUND A FLY
IN HIS LOBSTER BISQUE,
IT RESULTED IN THIS.

Now arrange the circled letters to form
the surprise answer, as suggested by the
above cartoon.

*Print answer
here*

JUMBLE®

Unscramble these four Jumbles, one letter to
each square, to form four ordinary words.

INBOS

CREMY

WROAND

ONEOLD

Lois, could
you press my
uniform?

Press it
yourself,
Superguy!

AFTER SEEING HOW
WRINKLED HIS SUIT WAS,
SUPERMAN WOULD
BECOME THIS.

Now arrange the circled letters to form
the surprise answer, as suggested by the
above cartoon.

Print answer here

JUMBLE®

Unscramble these four Jumbles, one letter to each square, to form four ordinary words.

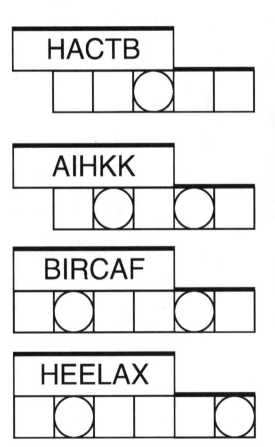

HACTB

AIHKK

BIRCAF

HEELAX

I've come all this way. I guess I don't have any choice but to pay.

Pay Entrance Fee Here

WHEN THE STATE PARK LEVIED A USAGE FEE FOR ITS TRAILS, HE FACED A ----

Now arrange the circled letters to form the surprise answer, as suggested by the above cartoon.

Print answer here

11

JUMBLE®

Unscramble these four Jumbles, one letter to each square, to form four ordinary words.

CKSUN

ACEBH

SCORAS

BOLUED

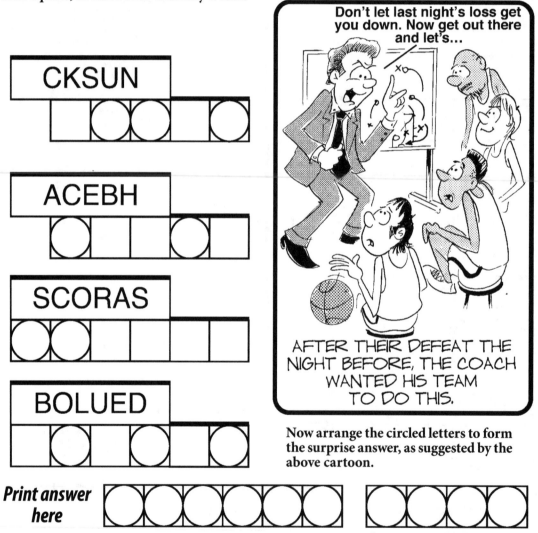

Don't let last night's loss get you down. Now get out there and let's...

AFTER THEIR DEFEAT THE NIGHT BEFORE, THE COACH WANTED HIS TEAM TO DO THIS.

Now arrange the circled letters to form the surprise answer, as suggested by the above cartoon.

Print answer here

JUMBLE®

Unscramble these four Jumbles, one letter to
each square, to form four ordinary words.

KACTR
◯◯◯□□

HRPOM
◯◯□□

UNSEFI
□◯◯□□◯

INVIED
◯□□□◯□

It's been nice without the guys here.

WHILE THE MEN
WERE AWAY,
THE WOMEN ----

Now arrange the circled letters to form
the surprise answer, as suggested by the
above cartoon.

*Print
answer
here* ◯◯◯◯◯◯ **THE** ◯◯◯◯

13

JUMBLE®

Unscramble these four Jumbles, one letter to
each square, to form four ordinary words.

COLAF

CEELT

FINNAT

WABREE

Today will be the best show I've ever
done. Because I'm good enough, I'm
smart enough, and, doggone it,
people like me!

WHEN HE TALKED TO
HIMSELF IN THE MIRROR,
HE TALKED
TO HIMSELF ---

Now arrange the circled letters to form
the surprise answer, as suggested by the
above cartoon.

Print
answer
here

- " " -

JUMBLE®

Unscramble these four Jumbles, one letter to
each square, to form four ordinary words.

FLUBF

KECOG

OCITEX

SOMPIE

I love playing
here on vacation.

The
water's so
blue!

HOYO
NUMERO
UNO

THEY TEED OFF
IN CANCUN TO
EXPERIENCE THE ---

Now arrange the circled letters to form
the surprise answer, as suggested by the
above cartoon.

*Print
answer
here*   " ⟨ ⟩⟨ ⟩⟨ ⟩⟨ ⟩ " ⟨ ⟩⟨ ⟩ ⟨ ⟩⟨ ⟩⟨ ⟩⟨ ⟩⟨ ⟩⟨ ⟩⟨ ⟩

JUMBLE®

Unscramble these four Jumbles, one letter to each square, to form four ordinary words.

USHEO

IYSTP

SONLAM

MOWSID

What do you mean you replaced me? How can you do that? I've been here for 20 years!

It wasn't my decision. Didn't they call you to let you know?

WJM 7

GETTING FIRED WAS THIS TO THE ANCHORMAN.

Now arrange the circled letters to form the surprise answer, as suggested by the above cartoon.

Print answer here

JUMBLE®

Unscramble these four Jumbles, one letter to
each square, to form four ordinary words.

FRAET

CONTH

TECANC

GURAJA

Just 15 minutes
a day and I'll be
lean and mean in a
month.

Are you
kidding me?

3000

WHEN IT CAME TO HER
HUSBAND'S PLAN TO
SUCCESSFULLY LOSE
WEIGHT, SHE THOUGHT
HE HAD THIS.

Now arrange the circled letters to form
the surprise answer, as suggested by the
above cartoon.

*Print answer
here* A

JUMBLE®

Unscramble these four Jumbles, one letter to
each square, to form four ordinary words.

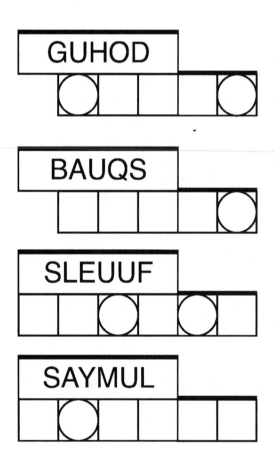

GUHOD

BAUQS

SLEUUF

SAYMUL

You look exhausted. Tell you
what. I'll go golfing tomorrow to
give you some peace and quiet.

AFTER A LONG DAY OF
PLANTING HEDGES,
SHE WAS THIS.

Now arrange the circled letters to form
the surprise answer, as suggested by the
above cartoon.

Print answer here

JUMBLE®

Unscramble these four Jumbles, one letter to each square, to form four ordinary words.

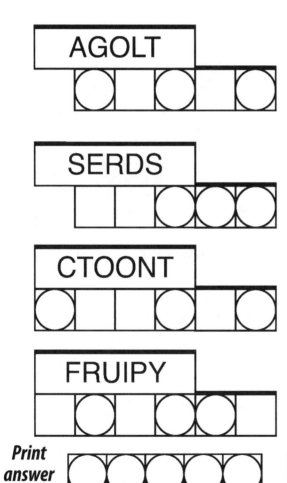

AGOLT

SERDS

CTOONT

FRUIPY

This pair of glasses was liked by more than 90% of the people who tried them out.

THE DESIGNS FOR THE NEW EYEGLASSES WERE CHOSEN AFTER THIS.

Now arrange the circled letters to form the surprise answer, as suggested by the above cartoon.

Print answer here

19

JUMBLE®

Unscramble these four Jumbles, one letter to
each square, to form four ordinary words.

TORLL

DENRT

GEWHIT

YALELV

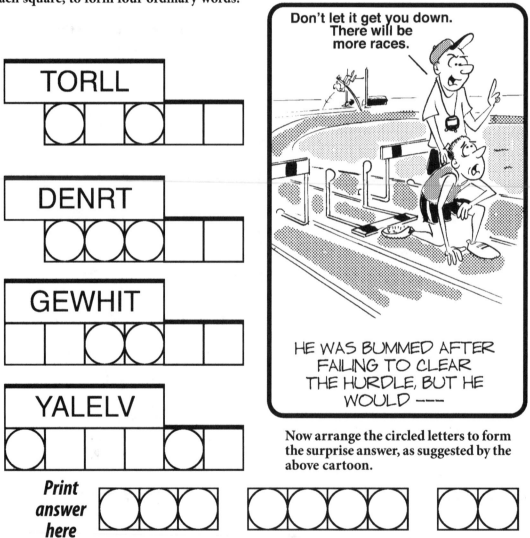

Don't let it get you down.
There will be
more races.

HE WAS BUMMED AFTER
FAILING TO CLEAR
THE HURDLE, BUT HE
WOULD ———

Now arrange the circled letters to form
the surprise answer, as suggested by the
above cartoon.

Print answer here

JUMBLE®

Unscramble these four Jumbles, one letter to each square, to form four ordinary words.

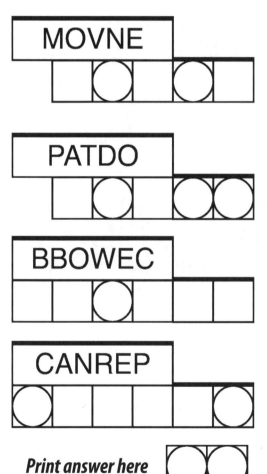

MOVNE

PATDO

BBOWEC

CANREP

Congratulations!
Your fromage
pizza is the
champ!

How could
that boring
pie win?

HIS CHEF'S AWARD-WINNING
PIZZA WAS SO GOOD THAT
IT COULDN'T ----

Now arrange the circled letters to form the surprise answer, as suggested by the above cartoon.

Print answer here

JUMBLE®

Unscramble these four Jumbles, one letter to
each square, to form four ordinary words.

DDEEG

CAYNF

CLAPID

TENYRG

Sweep it up.
We're diving.

Captain, we
need to get rid
of some trash.
Are we
surfacing
soon?

We need
some air
fresheners.

THE SUBMARINE
NEEDED A ---

Now arrange the circled letters to form
the surprise answer, as suggested by the
above cartoon.

Print
answer
here

JUMBLE®

Unscramble these four Jumbles, one letter to each square, to form four ordinary words.

RHILW

SUMYT

TOBCAL

SCAABU

Now arrange the circled letters to form the surprise answer, as suggested by the above cartoon.

Print answer here

JUMBLE®

Unscramble these four Jumbles, one letter to each square, to form four ordinary words.

MIGER

INTEW

BOWSET

SHYMIW

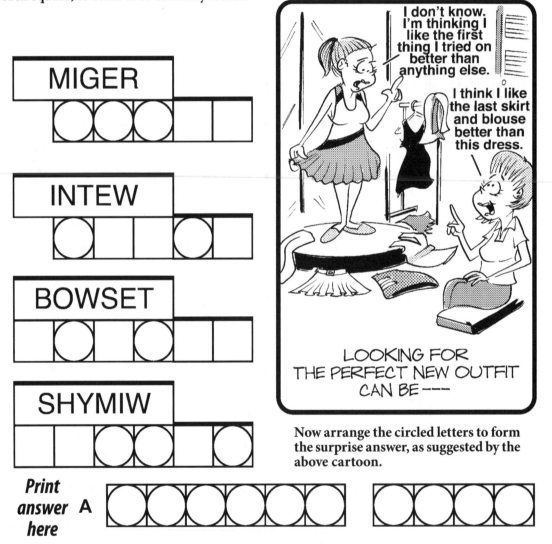

I don't know. I'm thinking I like the first thing I tried on better than anything else.

I think I like the last skirt and blouse better than this dress.

LOOKING FOR THE PERFECT NEW OUTFIT CAN BE ---

Now arrange the circled letters to form the surprise answer, as suggested by the above cartoon.

Print answer here   A ☐☐☐☐☐☐☐   ☐☐☐☐

JUMBLE®

Unscramble these four Jumbles, one letter to
each square, to form four ordinary words.

SERPS

SALCH

PENTUU

RXTEPE

She's so
fidgety
tonight.
I think we've
all forgotten
how to sleep.

Sleep!
What's
that?

WHEN THE BABY
WOULDN'T SLEEP, THE
PARENTS GOT---

Now arrange the circled letters to form
the surprise answer, as suggested by the
above cartoon.

Print answer here

JUMBLE®

Unscramble these four Jumbles, one letter to
each square, to form four ordinary words.

ZEDDO

CHANO

FACETF

RERVID

I really want to be
up front with you
from the start. My
passion is to
help people.

Wow!
That's
refreshing
to hear.

VOTE

THE POLITICIAN SPOKE
FRANKLY TO HIS DINNER
COMPANION BECAUSE
HE WAS A ---

Now arrange the circled letters to form
the surprise answer, as suggested by the
above cartoon.

*Print answer
here*

JUMBLE®

Kingdom

Daily Puzzles

JUMBLE®

Unscramble these four Jumbles, one letter to each square, to form four ordinary words.

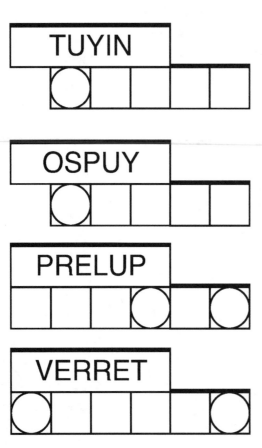

TUYIN

OSPUY

PRELUP

VERRET

Where's Dave?

Taking a nap to recover from the climb.

TAKING A NAP ON THE SUMMIT ALLOWED THE MOUNTAIN CLIMBER TO ---

Now arrange the circled letters to form the surprise answer, as suggested by the above cartoon.

Print answer here

JUMBLE®

Unscramble these four Jumbles, one letter to each square, to form four ordinary words.

ZAAME

GUNST

PLASIR

OPLAST

They both have great arms. I can't decide who will throw Sunday.

12

6

WHEN IT CAME TIME TO DECIDE ON A STARTING QUARTERBACK, THE COACH WAS ----

Now arrange the circled letters to form the surprise answer, as suggested by the above cartoon.

Print answer here

JUMBLE.

Unscramble these four Jumbles, one letter to
each square, to form four ordinary words.

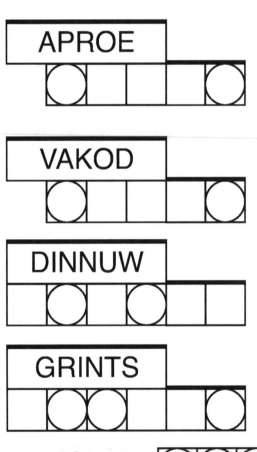

APROE

VAKOD

DINNUW

GRINTS

THE CROCODILE'S
COUSIN WAS A — — —

Now arrange the circled letters to form
the surprise answer, as suggested by the
above cartoon.

*Print answer
here*

JUMBLE®

Unscramble these four Jumbles, one letter to each square, to form four ordinary words.

USEOD

OPRUG

NEGNIE

OKRIEO

JPNY

Their mom over there was a super-model, too…and I think her mom, also.

THE SUPERMODEL TWINS SHOWED OFF THEIR ---

Now arrange the circled letters to form the surprise answer, as suggested by the above cartoon.

Print answer here

31

JUMBLE®

Unscramble these four Jumbles, one letter to each square, to form four ordinary words.

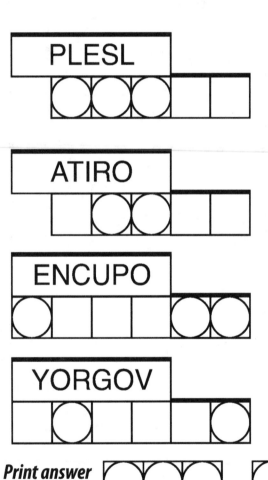

PLESL

ATIRO

ENCUPO

YORGOV

THANK YOU VETERANS!

AN IMPORTANT WAY TO COMPENSATE OUR VETERANS IS TO ---

Now arrange the circled letters to form the surprise answer, as suggested by the above cartoon.

Print answer here

Unscramble these four Jumbles, one letter to each square, to form four ordinary words.

BREEL

TOGAL

RALDIZ

SSALPH

Sign here, here, here, here, here...

You've got to move it.

WHEN KING KONG AGREED TO BUY THE EMPIRE STATE BUILDING, IT WAS A ---

Now arrange the circled letters to form the surprise answer, as suggested by the above cartoon.

Print answer here

32

JUMBLE®

Unscramble these four Jumbles, one letter to each square, to form four ordinary words.

FLUWA

HEWEL

LEBLUT

MOONIT

We're lucky he was so alert.

Aww! Just missed it.

92

4

Got it!

HE WAS ABLE TO RECOVER THE FUMBLE BECAUSE HE WAS ---

Now arrange the circled letters to form the surprise answer, as suggested by the above cartoon.

Print answer here

JUMBLE®

Unscramble these four Jumbles, one letter to each square, to form four ordinary words.

GANTE

DUNMO

OSLAIR

FAMEAL

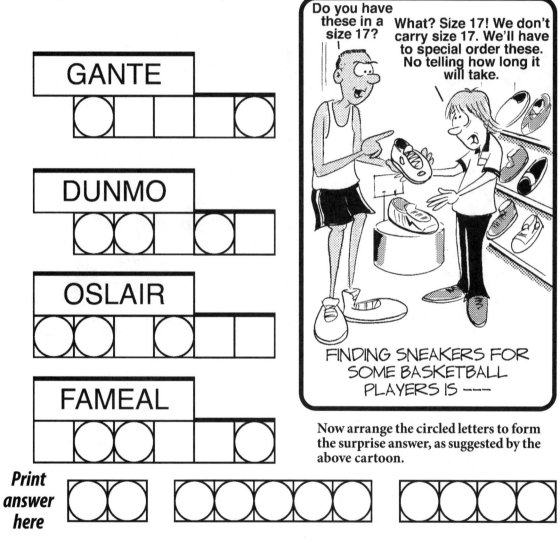

Do you have these in a size 17?

What? Size 17! We don't carry size 17. We'll have to special order these. No telling how long it will take.

FINDING SNEAKERS FOR SOME BASKETBALL PLAYERS IS ---

Now arrange the circled letters to form the surprise answer, as suggested by the above cartoon.

Print answer here

PUZZLE 34

JUMBLE®

Unscramble these four Jumbles, one letter to each square, to form four ordinary words.

DOYDL

GORNP

CASCUE

BATPRU

Now, it is very important that you don't mix these soils. The potting soil costs three times more than the topsoil.

TOP SOIL

TING SOIL

THE NURSERY OWNER TOLD HER NEW EMPLOYEE THE ---

Now arrange the circled letters to form the surprise answer, as suggested by the above cartoon.

Print answer here

36

JUMBLE®

Unscramble these four Jumbles, one letter to each square, to form four ordinary words.

TENIP

SLUKL

CREBAH

YENANO

Hey, Dave. We just re-signed our running back. Can you make sure he gets his signing bonus this week?

I'll cut him a check today.

BUFFALO'S NFL TEAM HIRED AN ACCOUNTANT TO DO THIS.

Now arrange the circled letters to form the surprise answer, as suggested by the above cartoon.

Print answer here

JUMBLE.

Unscramble these four Jumbles, one letter to
each square, to form four ordinary words.

RAWEY

TIBRO

PANEWO

HACTED

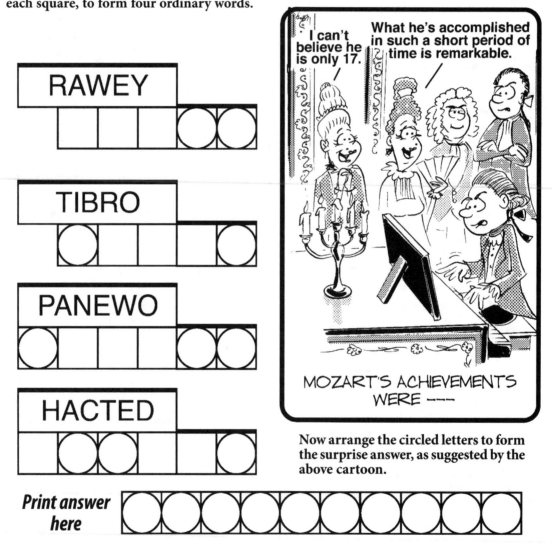

I can't believe he is only 17.

What he's accomplished in such a short period of time is remarkable.

MOZART'S ACHIEVEMENTS WERE ---

Now arrange the circled letters to form
the surprise answer, as suggested by the
above cartoon.

Print answer here

JUMBLE

Unscramble these four Jumbles, one letter to
each square, to form four ordinary words.

SEODU

IGILV

ROFNEZ

LAWPOL

People will be able to read
a book on a device like
this. It could hold
thousands of titles.

Where's the
keyboard?

AT ONE TIME, READING A
BOOK ON A NOOK, KINDLE
OR IPAD WAS A ----

Now arrange the circled letters to form
the surprise answer, as suggested by the
above cartoon.

*Print answer
here*

⬜◯◯◯◯◯ ⬜◯◯◯◯

JUMBLE®

Unscramble these four Jumbles, one letter to each square, to form four ordinary words.

ARCKO

MEVON

GEDDER

TENTIK

This guy doesn't just want to win, you know. He wants to bury you. Now put your eye back in and let him have it.

THE ZOMBIE BOXER'S MANAGER TOLD HIM TO ---

Now arrange the circled letters to form the surprise answer, as suggested by the above cartoon.

Print answer here

 '

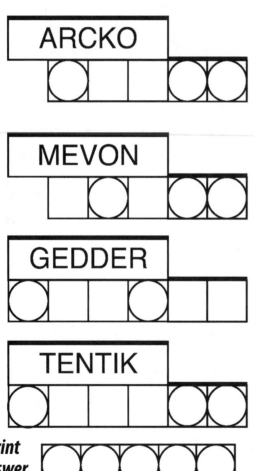

JUMBLE®

Unscramble these four Jumbles, one letter to
each square, to form four ordinary words.

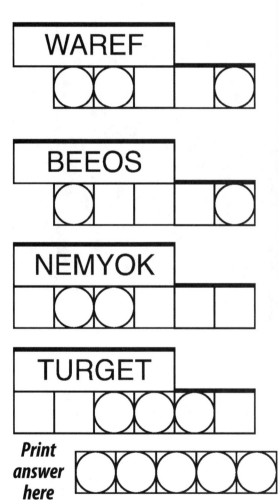

WAREF

BEEOS

NEMYOK

TURGET

Da da da.
I need to jot this
down.

BARRY MANILOW
DIDN'T WANT TO FORGET
HIS IDEA FOR A NEW SONG,
SO HE ----

Now arrange the circled letters to form
the surprise answer, as suggested by the
above cartoon.

**Print
answer
here**

JUMBLE®

Unscramble these four Jumbles, one letter to each square, to form four ordinary words.

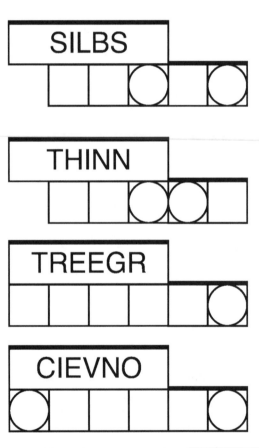

SILBS

THINN

TREEGR

CIEVNO

Come on, ladies!
Get those shelters built.
We've got a 5-mile
trail run before lunch.

THE
SCOUT OUTING
WAS ---

Now arrange the circled letters to form the surprise answer, as suggested by the above cartoon.

Print answer here " ◯◯ - ◯◯◯◯◯ "

JUMBLE®

Unscramble these four Jumbles, one letter to each square, to form four ordinary words.

HENTT

OUIDA

CUHRCN

MEHRMA

I can count on the trees to be bare every year by the last day of fall.

LEAVES FALLING OFF THE TREES EACH YEAR IS ----

Now arrange the circled letters to form the surprise answer, as suggested by the above cartoon.

Print answer here

" ☐☐☐☐☐☐ - ☐☐☐☐☐ "

43

JUMBLE®

Unscramble these four Jumbles, one letter to each square, to form four ordinary words.

NARWB

DEGEH

SODWIN

AUTRIL

We have over 500 beers available.

Wow! That's 499 more than my regular hangout. I'll have to try them all.

THE FANCY NEW PUB REALLY –––

Now arrange the circled letters to form the surprise answer, as suggested by the above cartoon.

Print answer here

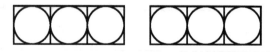

44

JUMBLE®

Unscramble these four Jumbles, one letter to each square, to form four ordinary words.

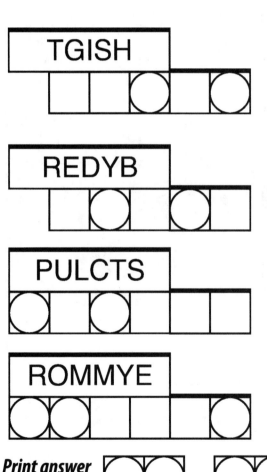

TGISH

REDYB

PULCTS

ROMMYE

I know we're early, but can we check in now?

You're in luck. Your room is ready now.

WHEN THEY ASKED THE OWNER OF THE INN IF THEY COULD CHECK IN EARLY, HE SAID ----

Now arrange the circled letters to form the surprise answer, as suggested by the above cartoon.

Print answer here

JUMBLE®

Unscramble these four Jumbles, one letter to each square, to form four ordinary words.

PUREP

KNURT

AUNLAN

CEHNAG

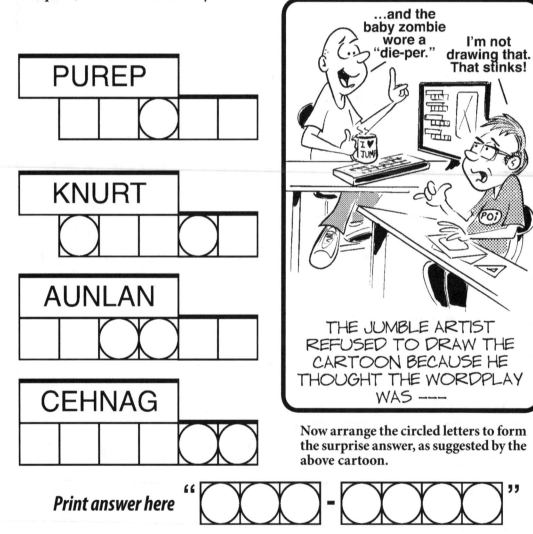

...and the baby zombie wore a "die-per."

I'm not drawing that. That stinks!

THE JUMBLE ARTIST REFUSED TO DRAW THE CARTOON BECAUSE HE THOUGHT THE WORDPLAY WAS ‒‒‒

Now arrange the circled letters to form the surprise answer, as suggested by the above cartoon.

Print answer here " ◯◯◯◯ - ◯◯◯◯◯ "

JUMBLE®

Unscramble these four Jumbles, one letter to each square, to form four ordinary words.

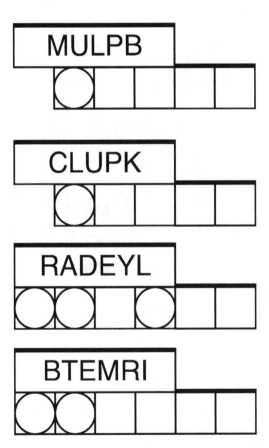

MULPB

CLUPK

RADEYL

BTEMRI

Blimey, miss! What happened to you?

I stumbled in front of a taxi.

EVERYTHING WAS GOING GREAT ON HER EUROPEAN VACATION UNTIL SHE ----

Now arrange the circled letters to form the surprise answer, as suggested by the above cartoon.

Print answer here

47

JUMBLE®

Unscramble these four Jumbles, one letter to
each square, to form four ordinary words.

FCSUF

PHUMT

CITTEK

FRODAF

I'll have to
look for your
address on
my map.

You don't have
GPS?
How old is this
car?

THE LIMO DRIVER HAD
BEEN WORKING FOR YEARS
BUT HE DIDN'T HAVE
MUCH TO ----

Now arrange the circled letters to form
the surprise answer, as suggested by the
above cartoon.

Print
answer
here

" ⬭⬭⬭⬭⬭⬭⬭⬭⬭⬭ " ⬭⬭

JUMBLE®

Unscramble these four Jumbles, one letter to each square, to form four ordinary words.

REOYF

ARNOY

CAFROT

GLITHF

THE NEW SHOE STORE WAS DOING QUITE WELL THANKS TO ALL THE ---

Now arrange the circled letters to form the surprise answer, as suggested by the above cartoon.

Print answer here

49

JUMBLE®

Unscramble these four Jumbles, one letter to
each square, to form four ordinary words.

IRROG

CINEM

DAXNEP

MULHEB

You haven't paid your
dues in more than six
months. You'll need to
talk to someone about
signing back up.

I'm so sorry.
I forgot all
about it.

Fishers Fitness

AFTER FORGETTING TO
PAY HIS GYM DUES, HE
NEEDED TO ---

Now arrange the circled letters to form
the surprise answer, as suggested by the
above cartoon.

Print answer here " ◯◯ - ◯◯◯◯◯◯ "

JUMBLE®

Unscramble these four Jumbles, one letter to each square, to form four ordinary words.

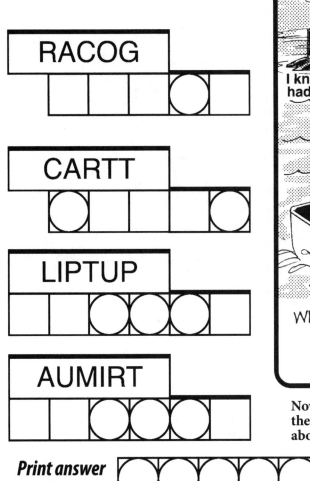

RACOG

CARTT

LIPTUP

AUMIRT

This is what you get. You deserve this. Enjoy your short cruise.

I know. I wish I hadn't done it.

ALCATRAZ EXPRESS

WHEN THE PRISONER WAS SHIPPED OFF TO ALCATRAZ, HE WENT ON A ----

Now arrange the circled letters to form the surprise answer, as suggested by the above cartoon.

Print answer here

JUMBLE.

Unscramble these four Jumbles, one letter to each square, to form four ordinary words.

LERED

CLEET

ALSURW

PODTEP

I like the peace and quiet at night.

Hopefully, the crew is getting rested up.

IT WAS QUIET ON THE SUBMARINE BECAUSE MOST OF THE CREW WAS IN ----

Now arrange the circled letters to form the surprise answer, as suggested by the above cartoon.

Print answer here A

JUMBLE®

Unscramble these four Jumbles, one letter to
each square, to form four ordinary words.

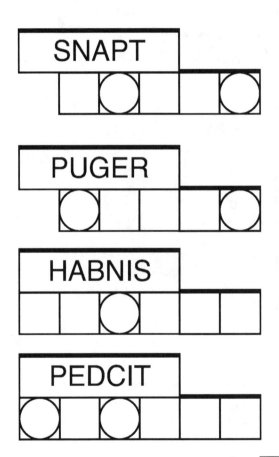

SNAPT

PUGER

HABNIS

PEDCIT

I almost broke
my neck!

I've used this
swing all my
life. Maybe
you're too
big!

AFTER THE ROPE
BROKE, HE ---

Now arrange the circled letters to form
the surprise answer, as suggested by the
above cartoon.

Print answer here

JUMBLE®

Unscramble these four Jumbles, one letter to each square, to form four ordinary words.

CNULH

PADAT

RANWOR

CLOPIE

Don't worry. You'll get the hang of it.

Aww! Not again!

HE TRIED TO TEACH HIS SON HOW TO FISH, BUT HIS SON COULDN'T ---

Now arrange the circled letters to form the surprise answer, as suggested by the above cartoon.

Print answer here

JUMBLE®

Unscramble these four Jumbles, one letter to
each square, to form four ordinary words.

MILBP

PENIT

HOXTAR

LAPTEL

RINGO STARR'S ALL-STARR DRUM KIT

I love it! I'll take it.

Hey! I wanted to buy that!

HE WANTED TO BUY THE
CLASSIC DRUM SET, BUT
SOMEONE ----

Now arrange the circled letters to form
the surprise answer, as suggested by the
above cartoon.

Print
answer
here

JUMBLE®

Unscramble these four Jumbles, one letter to
each square, to form four ordinary words.

SIRBK

LAVUT

CUREED

PAYRAL

I wouldn't start my day without
Jumble Java. Neither should you!

I want to buy
some of that.

She seems
to always be
on TV.

WHEN THE ACTRESS
STARTED APPEARING
IN COMMERCIALS, SHE
BECAME A ---

Now arrange the circled letters to form
the surprise answer, as suggested by the
above cartoon.

Print answer "⬭⬭⬭⬭-⬭⬭⬭⬭⬭⬭"
here

JUMBLE®

Unscramble these four Jumbles, one letter to each square, to form four ordinary words.

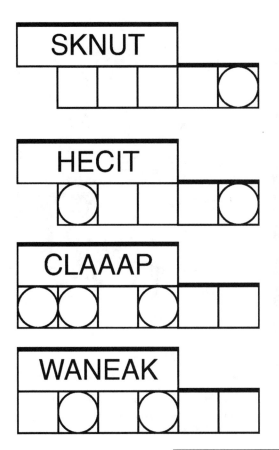

SKNUT

HECIT

CLAAAP

WANEAK

You gave it a great try.

This was a lot harder than I thought it would be.

CAKE BABY

CLOSED

OUT OF BUSINESS

SHE MISTAKENLY THOUGHT THAT OWNING A BAKERY WOULD BE A ----

Now arrange the circled letters to form the surprise answer, as suggested by the above cartoon.

Print answer here

JUMBLE®

Unscramble these four Jumbles, one letter to
each square, to form four ordinary words.

FARWD

BOATO

DRETNY

SUDSIC

Is that going to take long? It's hot in here.

No, not at all. I'll be done in a minute.

INSTALLING THE NEW
FAN AT THE GYM
WAS ---

Now arrange the circled letters to form
the surprise answer, as suggested by the
above cartoon.

Print answer here

58

JUMBLE®

Unscramble these four Jumbles, one letter to each square, to form four ordinary words.

OPRIR

TONEF

LUWTAN

SCECAS

Man!
I should have
moved to
Michigan.

DEATH VALLEY IS
SO HOT THANKS IN PART
TO ITS ---

Now arrange the circled letters to form
the surprise answer, as suggested by the
above cartoon.

Print answer " ☐☐☐ - ☐☐☐☐☐☐☐ "
here

JUMBLE®

Unscramble these four Jumbles, one letter to each square, to form four ordinary words.

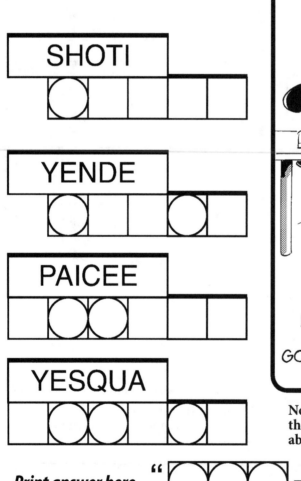

SHOTI

YENDE

PAICEE

YESQUA

Now arrange the circled letters to form the surprise answer, as suggested by the above cartoon.

Print answer here " ⃝⃝⃝ - ⃝⃝⃝⃝⃝ "

JUMBLE®

Unscramble these four Jumbles, one letter to
each square, to form four ordinary words.

REWAY

LIMYK

DEHDUL

LUPLAR

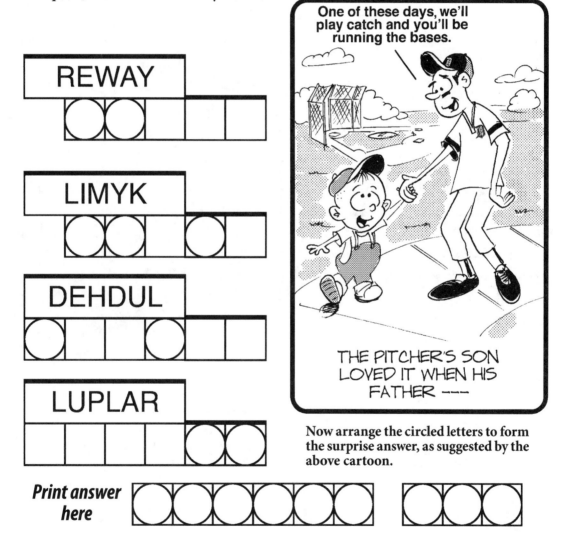

One of these days, we'll
play catch and you'll be
running the bases.

THE PITCHER'S SON
LOVED IT WHEN HIS
FATHER ---

Now arrange the circled letters to form
the surprise answer, as suggested by the
above cartoon.

**Print answer
here**

JUMBLE®

Unscramble these four Jumbles, one letter to each square, to form four ordinary words.

CHEFT

TREEX

LOYPIC

BAYTUE

My wife, Julie, just won the jackpot! She's lucky at slots and I'm lucky to be married to her.

I won! I won!

AFTER HIS WIFE STRUCK IT BIG ON A SLOT MACHINE, HE WAS HAPPY TO HAVE A ----

Now arrange the circled letters to form the surprise answer, as suggested by the above cartoon.

Print answer here

" ⬭⬭⬭⬭⬭⬭ " ⬭⬭⬭⬭

PUZZLE
61

JUMBLE®

Unscramble these four Jumbles, one letter to each square, to form four ordinary words.

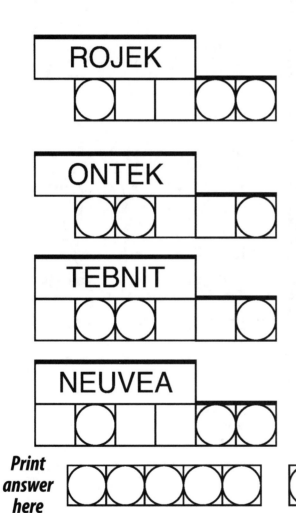

ROJEK

ONTEK

TEBNIT

NEUVEA

WHEN THEY DISCUSSED CREATING A COMPANY TO MAKE ARTIFICIAL KNEES, THEY PLANNED A ----

Now arrange the circled letters to form the surprise answer, as suggested by the above cartoon.

Print answer here

63

JUMBLE®

Unscramble these four Jumbles, one letter to
each square, to form four ordinary words.

XENAN

SERDS

TAHPAY

LIBGOE

Whoa! Babe!
Long time no
see. You look
great! Why'd
we ever break
up?

Didn't you
used to do
triathlons?

AFTER SEEING HER FORMER
HUSBAND FOR THE
FIRST TIME IN YEARS, SHE
WAS NOT ----

Now arrange the circled letters to form
the surprise answer, as suggested by the
above cartoon.

Print answer   "☐☐ - ☐☐☐☐☐☐☐☐"
here

JUMBLE

Unscramble these four Jumbles, one letter to
each square, to form four ordinary words.

ADRAW

GAMIE

CHENRD

ROPOYL

CAT CARTOON CONTEST

I love them all!

How'd you get
into this contest?

I love your
cartoon!

THE CARTOONING
COMPETITON
WOULD END ---

Now arrange the circled letters to form
the surprise answer, as suggested by the
above cartoon.

Print answer here ⬡⬡ ⬡ ⬡⬡⬡⬡

65

JUMBLE®

Unscramble these four Jumbles, one letter to each square, to form four ordinary words.

FORTN

PEWST

CIFLEK

TARREH

Here you go. I hope you liked your stay here in Salem a lot.

Thank you so much for printing out such a detailed receipt.

THE AUTHOR'S EXPENSES RELATED TO DOING RESEARCH FOR A NEW BOOK WOULD BE ----

Now arrange the circled letters to form the surprise answer, as suggested by the above cartoon.

Print answer here

JUMBLE®

Unscramble these four Jumbles, one letter to
each square, to form four ordinary words.

SOGEO

DYENE

CLUSPT

NOWWID

Did you know
that Death
Valley is one
of the hottest
and driest
places on
Earth?

Look at that
sea level.

Travel
Death Valley...
is 77.2 °F (25.1 °C)
Sea Level -282 Ft.

THEY STUDIED UP ON
DEATH VALLEY BEFORE
THEIR TRIP THERE SO THAT
THEY COULD GET THE – – –

Now arrange the circled letters to form
the surprise answer, as suggested by the
above cartoon.

Print answer here

JUMBLE.

Unscramble these four Jumbles, one letter to
each square, to form four ordinary words.

FINSF

DIRTH

TONLUD

TINNET

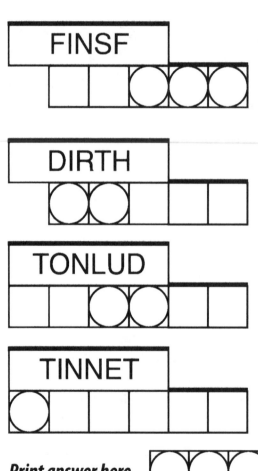

Remember,
baseball is 90%
mental and the
other half is
physical.

You guys
are the
best!

Go get 'em,
Mickey!

WHEN MICKEY MANTLE MADE
HIS DEBUT WITH THE NY
YANKEES ON 4-17-1951, HE
DID THIS WITH HIS NEW
TEAMMATES.

Now arrange the circled letters to form
the surprise answer, as suggested by the
above cartoon.

Print answer here

JUMBLE®

Unscramble these four Jumbles, one letter to each square, to form four ordinary words.

RANGD

FORDN

CESCIN

WESFET

You need to get your head examined if you think you can sell here!

I'm going to tell my mom on you if you don't leave!

LEMONADE 5¢

LEMONAID 5¢

TENSIONS MOUNTED BETWEEN THE LEMONADE SELLERS WHEN NEITHER OF THEM WOULD ----

Now arrange the circled letters to form the surprise answer, as suggested by the above cartoon.

Print answer here ⬡⬡⬡⬡⬡ ⬡⬡⬡⬡

69

JUMBLE®

Unscramble these four Jumbles, one letter to each square, to form four ordinary words.

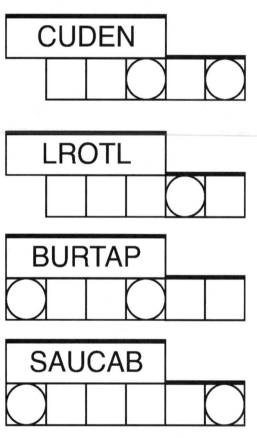

CUDEN

LROTL

BURTAP

SAUCAB

As you can see, I've named these bodies of water on the moon.

Tranquility

Serenity

He's mad!

I hope the man on the moon doesn't drown.

WHEN HE PROPOSED THAT THERE WERE OCEANS ON THE MOON, SOME PEOPLE THOUGHT IT WAS ----

Now arrange the circled letters to form the surprise answer, as suggested by the above cartoon.

Print answer here "◯◯◯◯◯-◯◯◯"

JUMBLE®

Unscramble these four Jumbles, one letter to
each square, to form four ordinary words.

LABEZ

PUCOH

MISLIE

TORRAY

That '70s Party

Like my
new do?

That is
so funny!

You are
cracking
me up!

EVERYONE THOUGHT
HER NEW WIG
WAS ---

Now arrange the circled letters to form
the surprise answer, as suggested by the
above cartoon.

*Print
answer
here*
"◯◯◯◯-◯◯◯◯◯◯◯◯"

JUMBLE®

Unscramble these four Jumbles, one letter to
each square, to form four ordinary words.

NAGIT

RAYAR

ROFLAM

SARMHY

What was
that?!
Who's
there!

THE "GARDEN" WAS
ALWAYS IN "DANGER"
BECAUSE IT WAS ----

Now arrange the circled letters to form
the surprise answer, as suggested by the
above cartoon.

Print answer here AN

JUMBLE®

Unscramble these four Jumbles, one letter to each square, to form four ordinary words.

EXPOY

DENEY

RAXMIT

CIYDIO

Oh, no! I should
have called a
professional. My car!

!

EVERYTHING WAS GOING
FINE AS HE CHOPPED
DOWN THE TREE UNTIL
THE ---

Now arrange the circled letters to form the surprise answer, as suggested by the above cartoon.

Print answer here " ◯◯◯ - ◯◯◯◯◯ "

73

JUMBLE®

Unscramble these four Jumbles, one letter to
each square, to form four ordinary words.

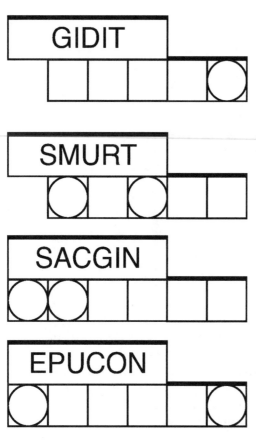

GIDIT

SMURT

SACGIN

EPUCON

I'll be right back.
No barking.

Rhonda's
Rugs

Rhonda's
Rugs

THE OWNER OF
THE RUG STORE
HAD ---

Now arrange the circled letters to form
the surprise answer, as suggested by the
above cartoon.

Print answer here

74

JUMBLE®

Unscramble these four Jumbles, one letter to
each square, to form four ordinary words.

HEVSO

BNALD

HENDID

DIFLED

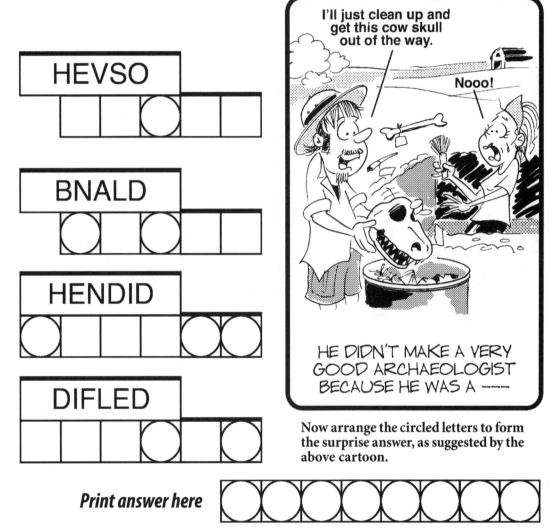

I'll just clean up and
get this cow skull
out of the way.

Nooo!

HE DIDN'T MAKE A VERY
GOOD ARCHAEOLOGIST
BECAUSE HE WAS A ---

Now arrange the circled letters to form
the surprise answer, as suggested by the
above cartoon.

Print answer here

JUMBLE®

Unscramble these four Jumbles, one letter to
each square, to form four ordinary words.

KEAAW

RYRUH

PIDTEC

TUNIOG

Stephan, you
should start
working out.

Huh?!

Anyone ever
call you Jeffy?

National Cartoonists Society
REUBEN AWARDS

MAD

Smile,
Dave!

Can everyone
move closer in?

WHEN ALL THE
CARTOONISTS GATHERED
FOR THE WEEKEND,
THEY WERE ----

Now arrange the circled letters to form
the surprise answer, as suggested by the
above cartoon.

Print
answer
here

76

JUMBLE®

Unscramble these four Jumbles, one letter to each square, to form four ordinary words.

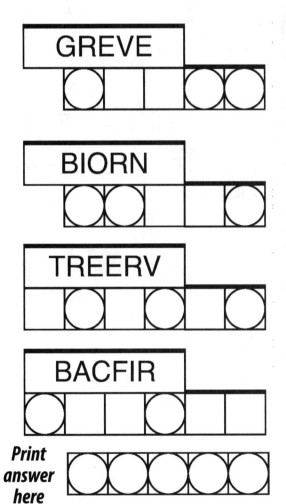

GREVE

BIORN

TREERV

BACFIR

This will make it easier to remember.

We must remember all those who have served and sacrificed.

CONGRESS DESIGNATED THAT MEMORIAL DAY WOULD ALWAYS BE THE LAST MONDAY IN MAY SO THAT WE'D ----

Now arrange the circled letters to form the surprise answer, as suggested by the above cartoon.

Print answer here

JUMBLE®

Unscramble these four Jumbles, one letter to each square, to form four ordinary words.

DANTS
○○□○

MOLBO
□○○○□

BARTIB
□○○□○

SIVINO
□□○□○

Hey! I was sitting there! I just went out for a second to feed the meter.

Hi ho. I don't want any trouble in here.

EVERYTHING WAS FINE AT THE AMPHIBIAN BAR UNTIL THE FROG SAT ON THE ----

Now arrange the circled letters to form the surprise answer, as suggested by the above cartoon.

Print answer here ○○○○○ ' ○ □ ○○○○○

JUMBLE®

Unscramble these four Jumbles, one letter to each square, to form four ordinary words.

NALST

XOCIT

ETOGOS

ATAFOL

What is the capital of Indiana? Which is larger, Texas or California? What ocean does Maryland border? What is the most populous city in Hawaii?

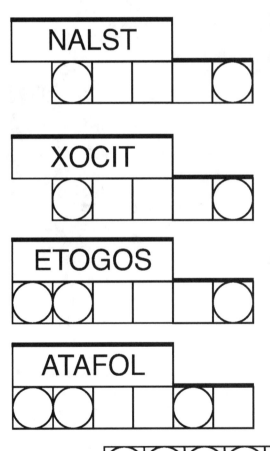

THE U.S. GEOGRAPHY TEACHER WANTED THE STUDENT TO ----

Now arrange the circled letters to form the surprise answer, as suggested by the above cartoon.

JUMBLE®

Unscramble these four Jumbles, one letter to each square, to form four ordinary words.

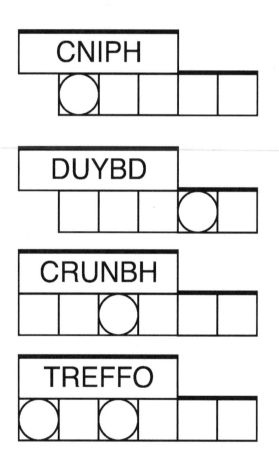

CNIPH

DUYBD

CRUNBH

TREFFO

This is horrible! I'm out of here.

I can't eat this!

THE FOOD AT THE RESTAURANT WAS SO BAD THAT CUSTOMERS WERE GETTING ----

Now arrange the circled letters to form the surprise answer, as suggested by the above cartoon.

Print answer here

80

JUMBLE®

Unscramble these four Jumbles, one letter to
each square, to form four ordinary words.

SUDOE

PRAAT

TINOGU

PERXET

Honey!
You can't just leave
me here!

Now we'll see
who's going
too slow.

HE BECAME ONE AFTER
TELLING HIS WIFE
HOW TO DRIVE.

Now arrange the circled letters to form
the surprise answer, as suggested by the
above cartoon.

*Print answer
here* A

JUMBLE®

Unscramble these four Jumbles, one letter to
each square, to form four ordinary words.

COTTE

REPSS

KABREY

HEVIRT

Mom is going
to be happy to
have these new
stairs.

WHEN THE IDENTICAL TWINS
BUILT THE STAIRCASE,
THEY BECAME ---

Now arrange the circled letters to form
the surprise answer, as suggested by the
above cartoon.

Print
answer
here

JUMBLE®

Unscramble these four Jumbles, one letter to each square, to form four ordinary words.

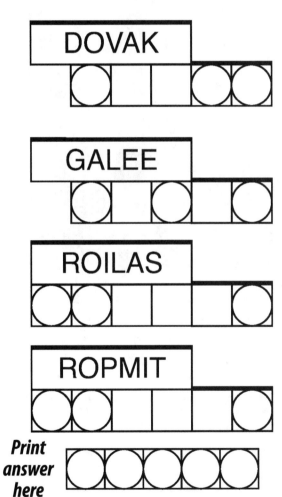

DOVAK

GALEE

ROILAS

ROPMIT

This is our plot. But that's not my husband's name!

I can't believe this! This is a serious blunder.

IMA GONER

SCOTT JAMES 1945-2013

JAMES SCOTT 1945-2013

THE MIX-UP AT THE CEMETERY WAS A ---

Now arrange the circled letters to form the surprise answer, as suggested by the above cartoon.

Print answer here

JUMBLE®

Unscramble these four Jumbles, one letter to each square, to form four ordinary words.

FENOT

RAWEA

SOMAIC

TONIMO

Now isn't this much more comfy than your old robe?

Wow! This is really plush.

2013 ROBES

BILL GATES BOUGHT THE NEW CASHMERE ROBE BECAUSE HE WANTED TO UPGRADE HIS ----

Now arrange the circled letters to form the surprise answer, as suggested by the above cartoon.

Print answer here " ◯◯◯◯◯◯◯◯◯ "

JUMBLE®

Unscramble these four Jumbles, one letter to each square, to form four ordinary words.

BOHCT

TUYOH

TEKTEL

PESCIT

What are we harvesting today?

BARRY'S BERRIES

I have no opinion. I'm taking the day off.

WHEN HE ASKED, "SHOULD WE HARVEST THE STRAWBERRIES OR THE BLUEBERRIES?" SHE SAID ---

Now arrange the circled letters to form the surprise answer, as suggested by the above cartoon.

Print answer here

JUMBLE®

Unscramble these four Jumbles, one letter to
each square, to form four ordinary words.

KANEL

OCTIX

LAVRUG

SHIRTT

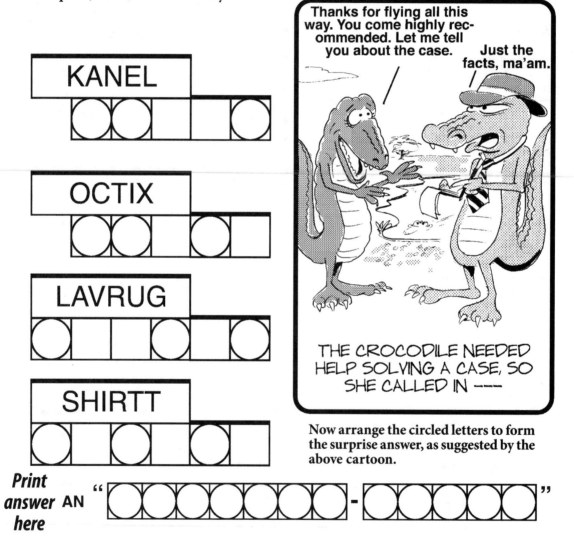

Thanks for flying all this
way. You come highly rec-
ommended. Let me tell
you about the case.

Just the
facts, ma'am.

THE CROCODILE NEEDED
HELP SOLVING A CASE, SO
SHE CALLED IN - - - -

Now arrange the circled letters to form
the surprise answer, as suggested by the
above cartoon.

Print
answer
here
AN " ☐☐☐☐☐☐☐☐-☐☐☐☐☐ "

JUMBLE®

Unscramble these four Jumbles, one letter to
each square, to form four ordinary words.

TOIDI

LATGO

TIMHER

TOBYAN

Hey! If you didn't want to
be eaten, you shouldn't
have gotten caught.

Let me go
or I'll cut off
your nose!

THE LOBSTER WAS THIS AT
THE PROSPECT OF
BECOMING SOMEONE'S
DINNER.

Now arrange the circled letters to form
the surprise answer, as suggested by the
above cartoon.

**Print answer
here**

JUMBLE®

Unscramble these four Jumbles, one letter to
each square, to form four ordinary words.

EAROP

FEYTH

EBUCON

MUCSAP

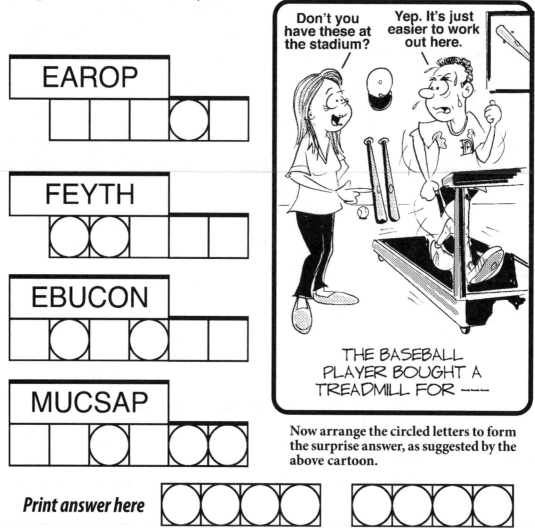

Don't you
have these at
the stadium?

Yep. It's just
easier to work
out here.

THE BASEBALL
PLAYER BOUGHT A
TREADMILL FOR ---

Now arrange the circled letters to form
the surprise answer, as suggested by the
above cartoon.

Print answer here

JUMBLE®

Unscramble these four Jumbles, one letter to
each square, to form four ordinary words.

PENIT

THIMG

HENTGL

DARITE

You just can't
expect a wire to
glow very long.

It can with the
right filament.
Here. Look at this.
I show that carbon
is the key.

HE DIDN'T BELIEVE IN THE
INVENTOR'S PLANS FOR THE
INCANDESCENT BULB, SO
EDISON ---

Now arrange the circled letters to form
the surprise answer, as suggested by the
above cartoon.

**Print
answer
here**

HIM

JUMBLE®

Unscramble these four Jumbles, one letter to
each square, to form four ordinary words.

CATYK

UIDAO

LAFDEW

LOGEIA

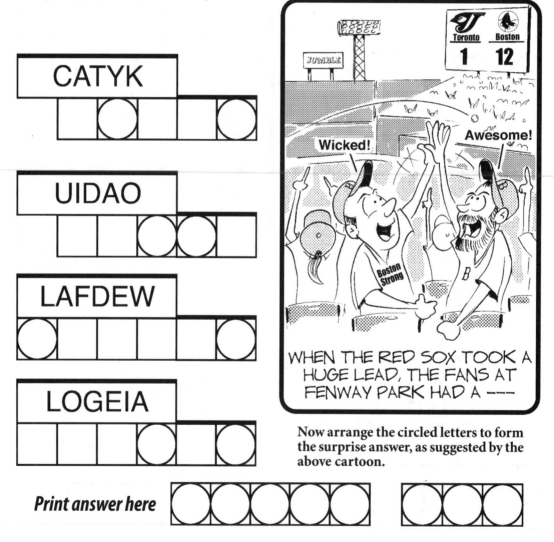

WHEN THE RED SOX TOOK A
HUGE LEAD, THE FANS AT
FENWAY PARK HAD A ---

Now arrange the circled letters to form
the surprise answer, as suggested by the
above cartoon.

Print answer here

JUMBLE®

Unscramble these four Jumbles, one letter to each square, to form four ordinary words.

IMOAX

RULBT

BLEEFE

OTELUT

I have to go out of town the end of next week. Would it be OK if we had your next lesson on Monday instead of Tuesday?

I can do that.

WHEN IT CAME TO SCHEDULING HER NEXT GYMNASTICS LESSON, THE STUDENT WAS ---

Now arrange the circled letters to form the surprise answer, as suggested by the above cartoon.

Print answer here

JUMBLE®

Unscramble these four Jumbles, one letter to each square, to form four ordinary words.

PALAH

KRUNT

REPNOS

MEEFLA

We're at port now, if you'd like to explore the city.

I need a nap.

I ate too much. I can't move.

AFTER THE BUFFET ABOARD THE CRUISE SHIP, EVERYONE CAME TO A ---

Now arrange the circled letters to form the surprise answer, as suggested by the above cartoon.

Print answer here

JUMBLE®

Unscramble these four Jumbles, one letter to
each square, to form four ordinary words.

POSIL

DALUT

WARLSP

RUTPIN

Finally.
Here's my
chance.

WHEN HE FINALLY HAD A
CHANCE TO GO AROUND
THE SLOW CAR, HE
COULDN'T ---

Now arrange the circled letters to form
the surprise answer, as suggested by the
above cartoon.

Print answer here

JUMBLE®

Unscramble these four Jumbles, one letter to each square, to form four ordinary words.

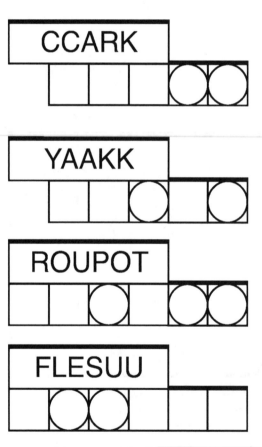

CCARK

YAAKK

ROUPOT

FLESUU

BUY 1 GET 5 FREE!

This is our biggest sales week of the year.

Wow! This is big.

THE 4TH OF JULY CAUSED SALES AT THE FIREWORKS STORE TO ----

Now arrange the circled letters to form the surprise answer, as suggested by the above cartoon.

Print answer here

94

JUMBLE®

Unscramble these four Jumbles, one letter to each square, to form four ordinary words.

SKKOI

TGLIH

BUPATE

NICTEE

Another grail of ale, Sir Bedivere?

It's good to hang out with you again, your majesty.

AFTER HE RETIRED, KING ARTHUR OPENED A ----

Now arrange the circled letters to form the surprise answer, as suggested by the above cartoon.

Print answer here " ⃝⃝⃝⃝⃝⃝ " ⃝⃝⃝⃝

95

JUMBLE®

Unscramble these four Jumbles, one letter to each square, to form four ordinary words.

LYODD

TALUF

VISNET

LINSAD

I just can't compete against the big builders.

Bob's Boats

That's too bad. I hate to see you close.

NO MATTER HOW HARD HE TRIED, HE JUST COULDN'T KEEP HIS BOAT-BUILDING BUSINESS ---

Now arrange the circled letters to form the surprise answer, as suggested by the above cartoon.

Print answer here

PUZZLE
95

JUMBLE®

Unscramble these four Jumbles, one letter to
each square, to form four ordinary words.

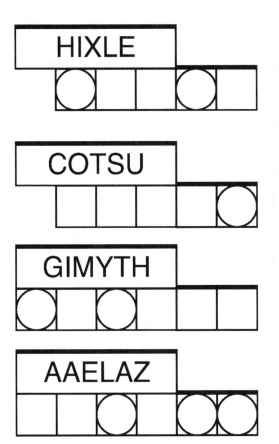

HIXLE

COTSU

GIMYTH

AAELAZ

HOME 1   VISITORS 1

JUMBLE

THE SOCCER MATCH
IN BANGKOK
WAS ---

Now arrange the circled letters to form
the surprise answer, as suggested by the
above cartoon.

Print answer here A "  "

97

JUMBLE®

Unscramble these four Jumbles, one letter to
each square, to form four ordinary words.

SURCO

CATHH

DOINIE

RACSEC

I'm going
to use the
new grip
you taught
me today.

Atta
boy!

THE BASEBALL TEAM'S
PITCHING INSTRUCTOR
LIVED IN ----

Now arrange the circled letters to form
the surprise answer, as suggested by the
above cartoon.

Print answer
here   A

98

JUMBLE®

Unscramble these four Jumbles, one letter to each square, to form four ordinary words.

LAMTE

KACOL

VEDNAT

LOBWIL

What is it, Lassie? You look down.

I'm just missing the old days. Remember when you fell down the well? Good times.

LASSIE WAS A BIT DEPRESSED AND FEELING ----

Now arrange the circled letters to form the surprise answer, as suggested by the above cartoon.

Print answer here " ⬤⬤⬤⬤⬤ - ⬤⬤⬤⬤⬤⬤ "

99

JUMBLE®

Unscramble these four Jumbles, one letter to
each square, to form four ordinary words.

FOLYT

GUWNS

DENCIU

PEHHNY

JUMBLE
AIR

I'd like
to be a
pilot.

Are you
kidding me?
You don't
even have
thumbs.

PORKY APPLIED FOR A JOB
AS AN AIRLINE PILOT, BUT
THE AIRLINE SAID ---

Now arrange the circled letters to form
the surprise answer, as suggested by the
above cartoon.

Print
answer
here

JUMBLE®

Unscramble these four Jumbles, one letter to each square, to form four ordinary words.

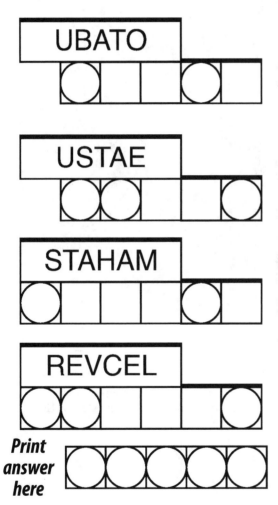

UBATO

USTAE

STAHAM

REVCEL

Time to wake up! You're going to be late.

How can she sleep so long? Why doesn't she have a clock?

THE TEENAGER CONSTANTLY OVERSLEEPING WAS ---

Now arrange the circled letters to form the surprise answer, as suggested by the above cartoon.

Print answer here

FOR

101

100

JUMBLE®

Unscramble these four Jumbles, one letter to
each square, to form four ordinary words.

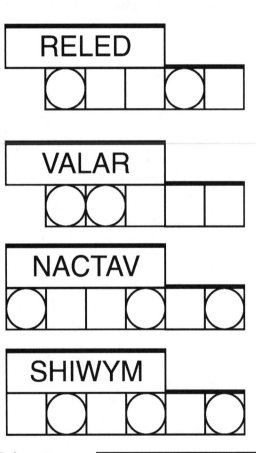

RELED

VALAR

NACTAV

SHIWYM

Hey, Garth,
it's Iron
Maiden!
Excellent!

I love
this
song!

THE IRONWORKERS
LISTENED TO ---

Now arrange the circled letters to form
the surprise answer, as suggested by the
above cartoon.

**Print answer
here**

102

JUMBLE®

Unscramble these four Jumbles, one letter to
each square, to form four ordinary words.

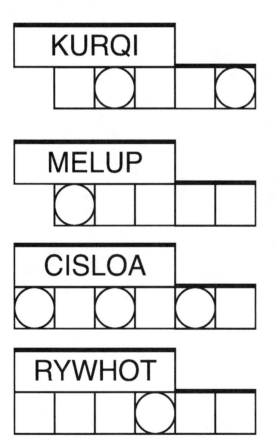

KURQI

MELUP

CISLOA

RYWHOT

Would you like to rebuy some chips?

Don't worry, Fred, I'm just holding on to your chips for now.

Where did my chips go?

COMPARED TO THE
COMPETITION, THE LOSING
POKER PLAYER DIDN'T ----

Now arrange the circled letters to form
the surprise answer, as suggested by the
above cartoon.

Print answer here

JUMBLE®

Unscramble these four Jumbles, one letter to each square, to form four ordinary words.

ROVGE

JEYNO

VIGLIN

MEBRUM

Cheeta. Me strong. You weak. Feel burn.

WHERE TARZAN WORKED OUT.

Now arrange the circled letters to form the surprise answer, as suggested by the above cartoon.

Print answer here AT THE ☐☐☐☐☐☐☐ ☐☐☐

JUMBLE®

Unscramble these four Jumbles, one letter to
each square, to form four ordinary words.

CNUBH

RACTA

DEALOD

RILFAY

I'm so sorry. I
don't know that
happened.

That's OK. Hey,
did you go to
Michigan, too?

THANKS TO THE
FENDER-BENDER, SHE MET
HER FUTURE HUSBAND ----

Now arrange the circled letters to form
the surprise answer, as suggested by the
above cartoon.

**Print answer
here**

JUMBLE®

Unscramble these four Jumbles, one letter to
each square, to form four ordinary words.

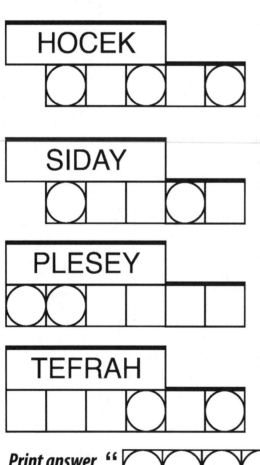

HOCEK

SIDAY

PLESEY

TEFRAH

Ready to go, Casey?
In G, on three.
1,2,3...

Whoa. Wait,
man. I have to
put some
strings on first.

SLIPPERY NOODLE INN.

STRINGS

the
warrior
kings

Jumble

EVEN THOUGH IT WAS
PLUGGED IN, THE ELECTRIC
GUITAR WITHOUT
STRINGS WAS ----

Now arrange the circled letters to form
the surprise answer, as suggested by the
above cartoon.

**Print answer
here** " ⬡⬡⬡⬡⬡ - ⬡⬡⬡⬡ "

JUMBLE®

Unscramble these four Jumbles, one letter to
each square, to form four ordinary words.

INYSH

REBIB

STILNP

NANTIF

Look. He's got a
big mouth like
your mother.

Don't let her
catch you saying
that.

THE NEWBORN FISH
SLEPT IN A ---

Now arrange the circled letters to form
the surprise answer, as suggested by the
above cartoon.

Print answer "◯◯◯◯ - ◯◯ - ◯◯◯"
here

JUMBLE®

Unscramble these four Jumbles, one letter to
each square, to form four ordinary words.

PATOD

ODORP

ROPENS

ECURSP

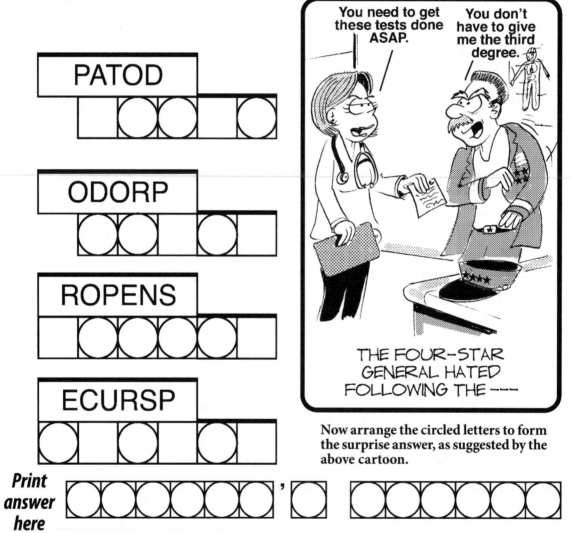

You need to get
these tests done
ASAP.

You don't
have to give
me the third
degree.

THE FOUR–STAR
GENERAL HATED
FOLLOWING THE ---

Now arrange the circled letters to form
the surprise answer, as suggested by the
above cartoon.

**Print
answer
here**

JUMBLE®

Unscramble these four Jumbles, one letter to
each square, to form four ordinary words.

HISUS

MUDHI

LISHEG

DOTDES

Hey, Mr. Kotter. We've
been here all day.
Can you let us
out early?

Oh! Oh!
Mr. Kotter!

I'm not sure
you've learned
anything if
you'd ask
me that.

A STUDENT HAD THE IDEA
THAT THEY SHOULD GET
OUT OF SCHOOL EARLY,
BUT THE TEACHER ----

Now arrange the circled letters to form
the surprise answer, as suggested by the
above cartoon.

Print
answer
here

JUMBLE®

Unscramble these four Jumbles, one letter to
each square, to form four ordinary words.

ROSYR

RABOV

CIBREK

TEMPIR

Look, man. I've showed you every guitar we have.

I'm not sure I like this one, either. Do you have any that sound more folksy?

HE WAS STRUGGLING TO
FIND A NEW GUITAR
BECAUSE HE WAS ----

Now arrange the circled letters to form
the surprise answer, as suggested by the
above cartoon.

Print answer here

JUMBLE®

Unscramble these four Jumbles, one letter to
each square, to form four ordinary words.

SPITY

LIPTO

SERDYS

CIERFE

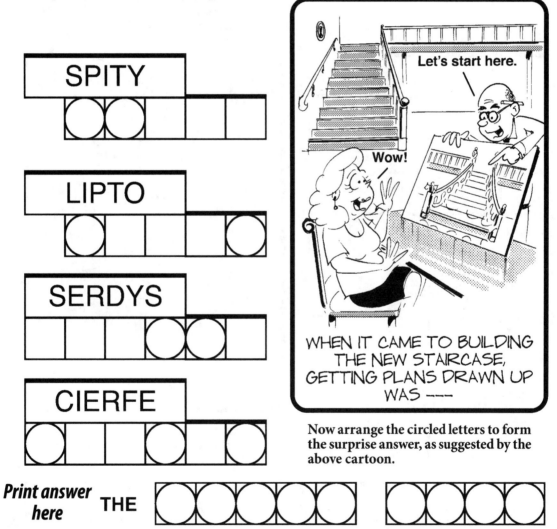

Let's start here.

Wow!

WHEN IT CAME TO BUILDING
THE NEW STAIRCASE,
GETTING PLANS DRAWN UP
WAS ---

Now arrange the circled letters to form
the surprise answer, as suggested by the
above cartoon.

**Print answer
here** THE

111

JUMBLE®

Unscramble these four Jumbles, one letter to
each square, to form four ordinary words.

CNIFH

TIDOT

ZEHEWE

NEMEAC

THE GUYS AT THE PIG
ROAST ---

Now arrange the circled letters to form
the surprise answer, as suggested by the
above cartoon.

**Print
answer
here**

112

JUMBLE ®

Unscramble these four Jumbles, one letter to
each square, to form four ordinary words.

CAINP

KARTC

VOLIJA

BUMEES

You can put
the lumber
behind the
house.

You have a lot
of room to
build.

THE AUSTRALIAN RANCHER
WAS BUILDING HIS
NEW BARN ----

Now arrange the circled letters to form
the surprise answer, as suggested by the
above cartoon.

Print answer here

113

JUMBLE®

Unscramble these four Jumbles, one letter to
each square, to form four ordinary words.

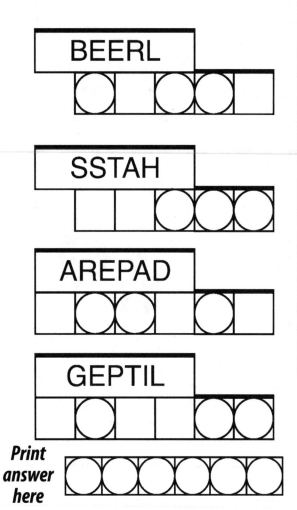

BEERL

SSTAH

AREPAD

GEPTIL

Wow! Did
you see
that?

No one is
going to be
able to beat
that!

THE WEIGHTLIFTER'S
NEW WORLD
RECORD ----

Now arrange the circled letters to form
the surprise answer, as suggested by the
above cartoon.

**Print
answer
here**

JUMBLE®

Unscramble these four Jumbles, one letter to each square, to form four ordinary words.

PONIA

DEEUL

BLADLA

YONWAH

I heard about this. It's better than I thought.

It's so big and beautiful!

WHEN THE FIRST SETTLERS SAW THE GRAND CANYON, THEY SAID ———

Now arrange the circled letters to form the surprise answer, as suggested by the above cartoon.

Print answer here

"⬡⬡⬡" ⬡⬡⬡ ⬡⬡⬡⬡⬡⬡

JUMBLE®

Unscramble these four Jumbles, one letter to each square, to form four ordinary words.

RUMLE

ROFOG

SICANO

RATNYP

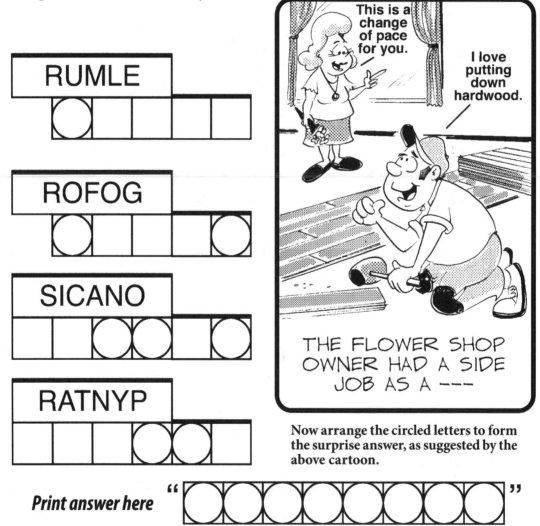

This is a change of pace for you.

I love putting down hardwood.

THE FLOWER SHOP OWNER HAD A SIDE JOB AS A ---

Now arrange the circled letters to form the surprise answer, as suggested by the above cartoon.

Print answer here " ◯◯◯◯◯◯◯◯◯ "

JUMBLE®

Unscramble these four Jumbles, one letter to each square, to form four ordinary words.

KEAAW

COFER

WRYLAM

NIZHET

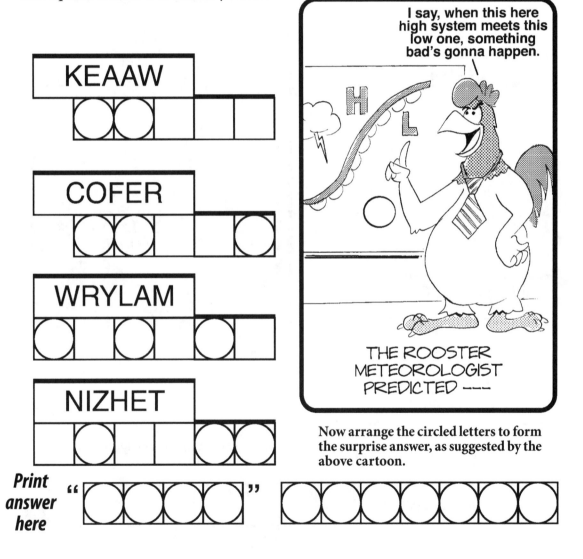

I say, when this here high system meets this low one, something bad's gonna happen.

THE ROOSTER METEOROLOGIST PREDICTED ----

Now arrange the circled letters to form the surprise answer, as suggested by the above cartoon.

Print answer here

" ⃝⃝⃝⃝ " ⃝⃝⃝⃝⃝⃝⃝

JUMBLE®

Unscramble these four Jumbles, one letter to each square, to form four ordinary words.

SLUPH

EXPIL

MOHFAT

RITREW

One of these days, this will all be yours.

This tie is choking me.

HIS FATHER WANTED HIM TO BECOME A TAILOR, BUT THE PROSPECT DIDN'T ----

Now arrange the circled letters to form the surprise answer, as suggested by the above cartoon.

Print answer here

JUMBLE®

Unscramble these four Jumbles, one letter to each square, to form four ordinary words.

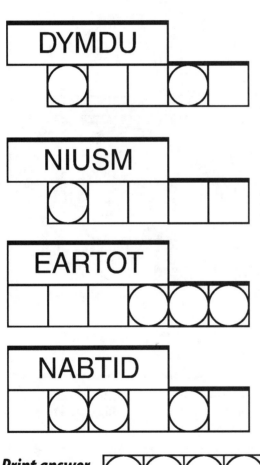

DYMDU

NIUSM

EARTOT

NABTID

The building is going up fast!

Their income will go up, too.

WHEN THE U.S. GOVERNMENT DECIDED TO EXPAND COIN PRODUCTION TO DENVER, THEY ---

Now arrange the circled letters to form the surprise answer, as suggested by the above cartoon.

Print answer here

119

JUMBLE®

Unscramble these four Jumbles, one letter to
each square, to form four ordinary words.

NACFY

GURYB

TELTES

LEBTAL

It's too big to
fit in the shot.

THE TOWER IN PARIS
WAS AN ---

Now arrange the circled letters to form
the surprise answer, as suggested by the
above cartoon.

Print answer here

JUMBLE®

Unscramble these four Jumbles, one letter to each square, to form four ordinary words.

DAIMT

HACSO

KORIOE

DURRED

I'm sorry. Your card has been declined and I have to destroy it.

What! You can't buy me the purse? Are you broke?

THE MAN WHO WASN'T AS WEALTHY AS HE LED PEOPLE TO BELIEVE WAS ----

Now arrange the circled letters to form the surprise answer, as suggested by the above cartoon.

Print answer here

JUMBLE®

Unscramble these four Jumbles, one letter to each square, to form four ordinary words.

LORAY

CANET

GAHNEC

SPIRCT

Butterscotch, behave! Now, let these children ride you.

Can we all ride him at the same time?

THE PONY WITH THE NEGATIVE ATTITUDE WAS ---

Now arrange the circled letters to form the surprise answer, as suggested by the above cartoon.

Print answer here   A   " ⬡⬡⬡⬡⬡ - ⬡⬡⬡⬡⬡ "

JUMBLE®

Unscramble these four Jumbles, one letter to each square, to form four ordinary words.

CRIKT

DURGA

KONIVE

YEILED

You cannot be serious!

The only thing you're going to serve is time.

$500

THE MAN WHO SOLD FAKE TENNIS EQUIPMENT ONLINE WAS CHARGED WITH ----

Now arrange the circled letters to form the surprise answer, as suggested by the above cartoon.

Print answer here

JUMBLE®

Unscramble these four Jumbles, one letter to
each square, to form four ordinary words.

WELLD

LIYLH

SUMOFA

REBHAC

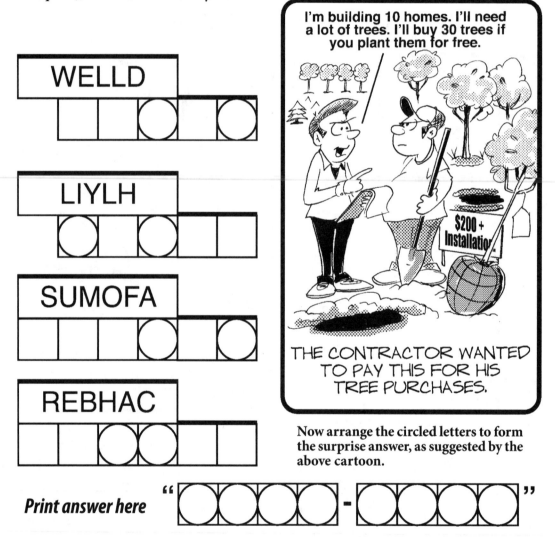

I'm building 10 homes. I'll need a lot of trees. I'll buy 30 trees if you plant them for free.

$200 + Installation

THE CONTRACTOR WANTED
TO PAY THIS FOR HIS
TREE PURCHASES.

Now arrange the circled letters to form
the surprise answer, as suggested by the
above cartoon.

Print answer here " ⭘⭘⭘⭘⭘ - ⭘⭘⭘⭘ "

PUZZLE
123

JUMBLE®

Unscramble these four Jumbles, one letter to each square, to form four ordinary words.

DOORE

SIRBK

CICOIN

RIPYAC

HIS TOUR OF ALCATRAZ TURNED INTO THIS WHEN HE FELL DOWN THE STAIRS.

Now arrange the circled letters to form the surprise answer, as suggested by the above cartoon.

Print answer here A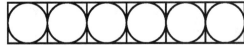

JUMBLE®

Unscramble these four Jumbles, one letter to each square, to form four ordinary words.

OGAME

KIRTC

CAUTIQ

GAHRAN

We're ready! Let's do this!

Let's go! First order up! Two scrambled eggs.

THE COOKS AT THE NEW BREAKFAST RESTAURANT WERE READY TO ---

Now arrange the circled letters to form the surprise answer, as suggested by the above cartoon.

Print answer here

JUMBLE®

Unscramble these four Jumbles, one letter to
each square, to form four ordinary words.

CINME

BOHYB

VILHAS

BUSDAR

WHEN THE YOUNG SHEEP
FOUGHT OVER THEIR
SLEEPING ARRANGEMENTS,
IT WAS ---

Now arrange the circled letters to form
the surprise answer, as suggested by the
above cartoon.

Print answer here " ☐☐☐ - ☐☐☐☐ "

JUMBLE®

Unscramble these four Jumbles, one letter to each square, to form four ordinary words.

CRODH

SOTDO

RIFMAF

WOTDAR

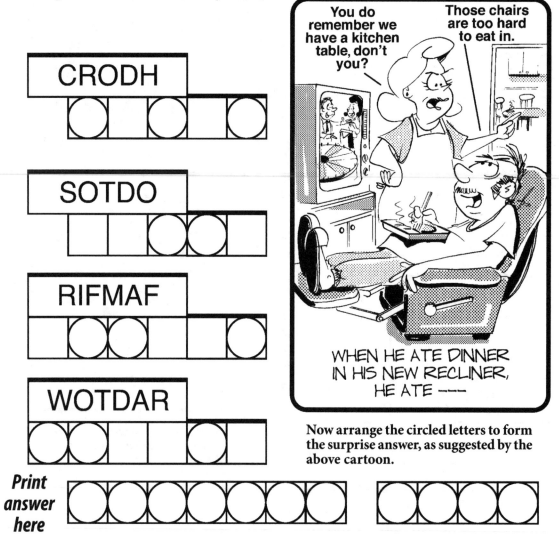

You do remember we have a kitchen table, don't you?

Those chairs are too hard to eat in.

WHEN HE ATE DINNER IN HIS NEW RECLINER, HE ATE ---

Now arrange the circled letters to form the surprise answer, as suggested by the above cartoon.

Print answer here

JUMBLE®

Unscramble these four Jumbles, one letter to each square, to form four ordinary words.

AGEMO

LOYHL

NASEOS

RADTIF

I've been doing this too long. It's the retiree's life for me.

You have lost your step.

THE PIRATE WAS READY TO RETIRE BECAUSE HE WAS ----

Now arrange the circled letters to form the surprise answer, as suggested by the above cartoon.

Print answer here

JUMBLE®

Unscramble these four Jumbles, one letter to
each square, to form four ordinary words.

LIPPU

VOBEA

RUBUNA

CLONUK

We're losing
height.
Are we out
of gas?

Don't worry.
I have a spare
tank. We'll be
aloft again
shortly.

THE HOT-AIR BALLOON
SANK AFTER THEY RAN OUT
OF FUEL, BUT HE HAD A ----

Now arrange the circled letters to form
the surprise answer, as suggested by the
above cartoon.

Print
answer
here

◯◯◯◯◯ - ◯◯   ◯◯◯◯

JUMBLE®

Unscramble these four Jumbles, one letter to
each square, to form four ordinary words.

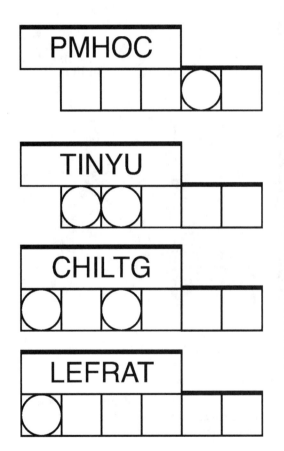

PMHOC

TINYU

CHILTG

LEFRAT

Are you kidding me? You couldn't
move 10 feet farther away?

AFTER WALKING THROUGH
THE SMOKERS TO GET
INSIDE, SHE WAS ----

Now arrange the circled letters to form
the surprise answer, as suggested by the
above cartoon.

Print answer here

JUMBLE®

Unscramble these four Jumbles, one letter to each square, to form four ordinary words.

LUMPP

DEYES

KRUNSH

DEAGAN

Did you see the news about our new flavor?

It made the front page.

Do you have the Jumble in there?

THE ICE CREAM PARLOR'S WEEKLY NEWSLETTER WAS THE ---

Now arrange the circled letters to form the surprise answer, as suggested by the above cartoon.

Print answer here " ◯◯◯◯◯◯ " ◯◯◯◯◯

JUMBLE

Unscramble these four Jumbles, one letter to each square, to form four ordinary words.

SHHRA

RABOV

NEOSAS

CAFROT

So, what do you think?

Are you kidding me? It's not Halloween.

AFTER SEEING HIS IDENTICAL TWIN'S NEW LOOK, HE SAID ---

Now arrange the circled letters to form the surprise answer, as suggested by the above cartoon.

Print answer here ⬡⬡ , ⬡⬡⬡⬡⬡⬡⬡

JUMBLE®

Unscramble these four Jumbles, one letter to
each square, to form four ordinary words.

ALEGI

DOLDY

CONIEM

VEDRIT

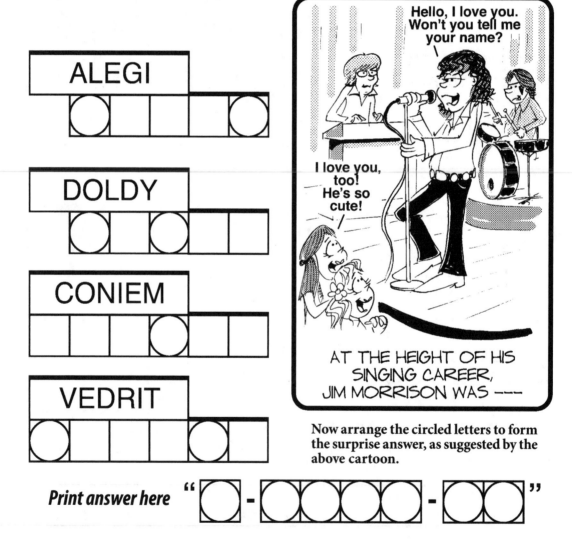

Hello, I love you.
Won't you tell me
your name?

I love you,
too!
He's so
cute!

AT THE HEIGHT OF HIS
SINGING CAREER,
JIM MORRISON WAS ----

Now arrange the circled letters to form
the surprise answer, as suggested by the
above cartoon.

Print answer here "◯ - ◯◯◯◯ - ◯◯"

JUMBLE®

Unscramble these four Jumbles, one letter to each square, to form four ordinary words.

KNAHT

AGGUE

CISNEK

NIWREN

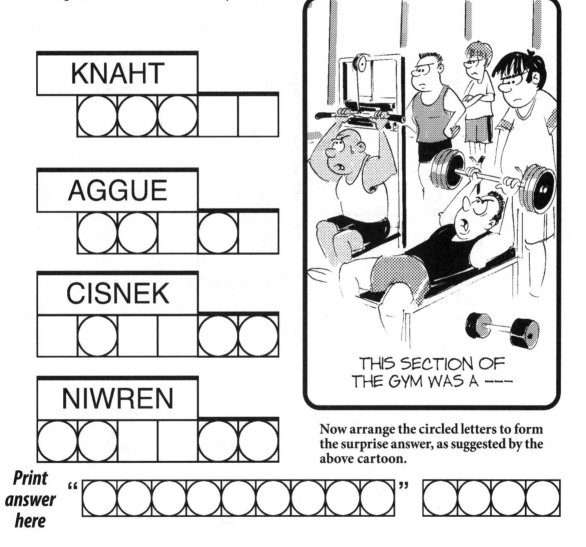

THIS SECTION OF
THE GYM WAS A ----

Now arrange the circled letters to form the surprise answer, as suggested by the above cartoon.

Print answer here " ◯◯◯◯◯◯◯◯◯◯ " ◯◯◯◯

JUMBLE®

Unscramble these four Jumbles, one letter to each square, to form four ordinary words.

NIXTO

YECDA

CCRUHH

COBNEK

Here you go. Now it's your turn.

FIVE ALARM WINGS

SHE WAS GOING TO TRY THE SPICY HOT WINGS, BUT SHE ----

Now arrange the circled letters to form the surprise answer, as suggested by the above cartoon.

Print answer here

JUMBLE®

Unscramble these four Jumbles, one letter to each square, to form four ordinary words.

CNUPH

NIDYK

NOPHOC

VEEBAR

I've got leverage on you.

THE ARM WRESTLER WAS ABOUT TO WIN BECAUSE HE HAD THE ---

Now arrange the circled letters to form the surprise answer, as suggested by the above cartoon.

Print answer here

JUMBLE®

Unscramble these four Jumbles, one letter to each square, to form four ordinary words.

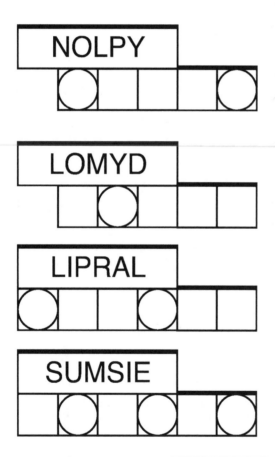

NOLPY

LOMYD

LIPRAL

SUMSIE

Ms. Helen, I'm lost on this geography homework.

Let's see what the problem is, Homer.

THE CYCLOPS TEACHER HAD JUST ----

Now arrange the circled letters to form the surprise answer, as suggested by the above cartoon.

Print answer here

JUMBLE®

Unscramble these four Jumbles, one letter to each square, to form four ordinary words.

STOIH

GEERM

YALGAX

SIFUNO

So, what's up, Doc?

Is th-th-th-that's all for me?

You really wrenched it.

PORKY HAD TO LEAVE THE BASKETBALL GAME AFTER HE INJURED HIS ---

Now arrange the circled letters to form the surprise answer, as suggested by the above cartoon.

Print answer here

139

JUMBLE®

Unscramble these four Jumbles, one letter to each square, to form four ordinary words.

BAHIT

SEGUT

TOPNET

DEEMLY

It doesn't get any nicer than this.

It's so beautiful here.

THEY WATCHED THE SUN GO DOWN FROM THE BEACH BECAUSE IT WAS A PERFECT ----

Now arrange the circled letters to form the surprise answer, as suggested by the above cartoon.

Print answer here

140

JUMBLE®

Unscramble these four Jumbles, one letter to each square, to form four ordinary words.

CANET

MIYLF

RETSOE

BIFAUL

Where did you get all of those?

Some of these were your great-grandfather's.

This was my father's favorite one.

HIS FATHER'S NECKWEAR COLLECTION WAS FULL OF ---

Now arrange the circled letters to form the surprise answer, as suggested by the above cartoon.

Print answer here

141

JUMBLE®

Unscramble these four Jumbles, one letter to each square, to form four ordinary words.

PONER

DIRTH

SADHIR

FABLEF

FEEDING THE HAWKS, VULTURES AND OWLS AT THE ZOO WAS SOMETIMES ----

Now arrange the circled letters to form the surprise answer, as suggested by the above cartoon.

Print answer here

142

Unscramble these four Jumbles, one letter to each square, to form four ordinary words.

LESTY

ROSIV

NUMMIE

MAGGIN

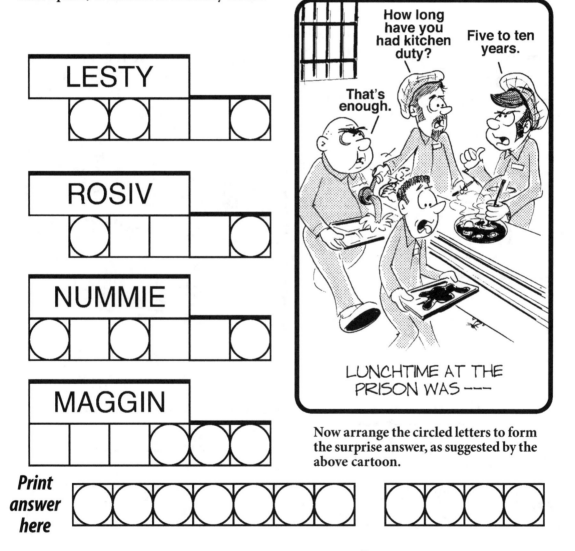

How long have you had kitchen duty?

Five to ten years.

That's enough.

LUNCHTIME AT THE PRISON WAS ----

Now arrange the circled letters to form the surprise answer, as suggested by the above cartoon.

Print answer here

JUMBLE®

Unscramble these four Jumbles, one letter to each square, to form four ordinary words.

SEPIO

GEDDO

NARPYT

RISKHN

We're sorry, but you just don't have any city planning experience.

Thank you for your time.

But, I really wanted the seat.

HOYT CITY COUNCIL

HOPING TO FILL THE SEAT OF THE DISGRACED COUNCILMAN, HE WAS ----

Now arrange the circled letters to form the surprise answer, as suggested by the above cartoon.

Print answer here

◯◯◯ - ◯◯◯◯◯◯◯◯◯

JUMBLE®

Unscramble these four Jumbles, one letter to
each square, to form four ordinary words.

SNUGW

SAYID

VELOVE

YMETSS

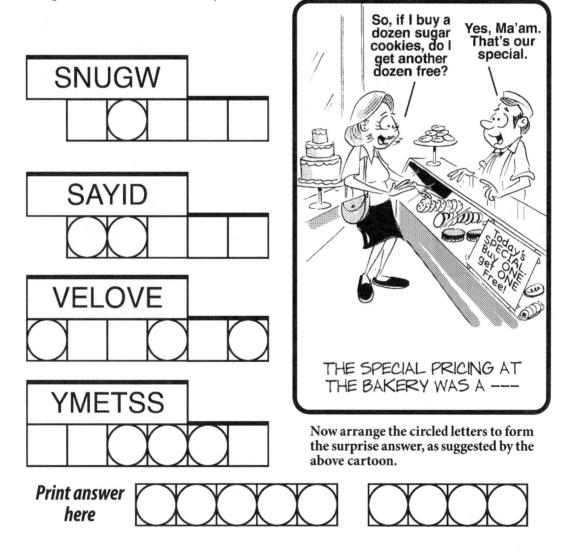

So, if I buy a dozen sugar cookies, do I get another dozen free?

Yes, Ma'am. That's our special.

Today's SPECIAL. Buy ONE. get ONE Free!

THE SPECIAL PRICING AT
THE BAKERY WAS A ----

Now arrange the circled letters to form
the surprise answer, as suggested by the
above cartoon.

Print answer here

JUMBLE®

Unscramble these four Jumbles, one letter to
each square, to form four ordinary words.

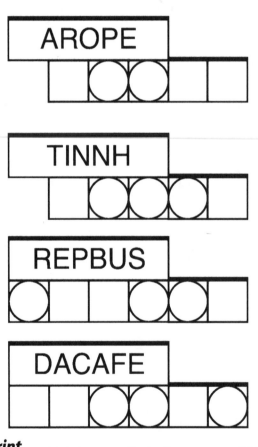

AROPE

TINNH

REPBUS

DACAFE

Good. You're home. I
need you to plant the
flowers, weed the
garden and take Spot
for a walk.

Are you
kidding me?
Can't I just
sit here by
myself for a
while?

AFTER A LONG DAY
WORKING AT THE CEMETERY,
THE GROUNDSKEEPER
WISHED HE COULD – – –

Now arrange the circled letters to form
the surprise answer, as suggested by the
above cartoon.

Print
answer
here

146

JUMBLE®

Unscramble these four Jumbles, one letter to each square, to form four ordinary words.

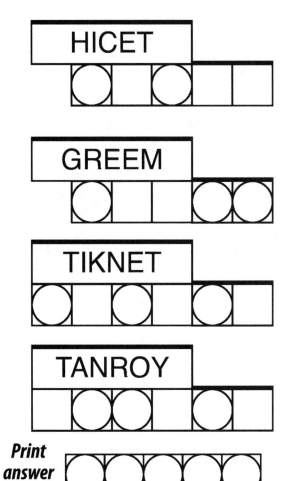

HICET

GREEM

TIKNET

TANROY

καφετέρια

Πιτσαρία Νικ

I have no idea what that says.

Τι όμορφη μέρα.

Πολλά τουριστικά σήμερα

I'll look it up.

THE TOURISTS WERE CONFUSED IN ATHENS BECAUSE EVERYTHING WAS ---

Now arrange the circled letters to form the surprise answer, as suggested by the above cartoon.

Print answer here

JUMBLE®

Unscramble these four Jumbles, one letter to each square, to form four ordinary words.

RAATP

GEDDO

NOLFYD

RECWUF

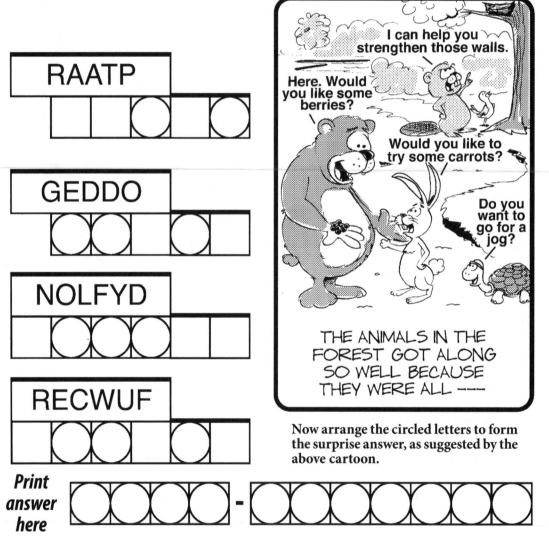

I can help you strengthen those walls.

Here. Would you like some berries?

Would you like to try some carrots?

Do you want to go for a jog?

THE ANIMALS IN THE FOREST GOT ALONG SO WELL BECAUSE THEY WERE ALL ----

Now arrange the circled letters to form the surprise answer, as suggested by the above cartoon.

Print answer here

☐☐☐☐ - ☐☐☐☐☐☐☐☐

JUMBLE®

Unscramble these four Jumbles, one letter to each square, to form four ordinary words.

FUINT

AGBYG

PANIDU

COIYDI

I've cut out the middleman. That's why they are so cheap. How many would you like?

That's not how you spell, "Prada."

PREDA $40

THE STREET VENDOR TOLD HER IT WAS AN AUTHENTIC HANDBAG, BUT SHE WASN'T ----

Now arrange the circled letters to form the surprise answer, as suggested by the above cartoon.

Print answer here

JUMBLE ®

Unscramble these four Jumbles, one letter to
each square, to form four ordinary words.

LEPSL

XOINT

RONCEE

CENLAG

It is this court's decision
that for the many crimes
that you've committed
and that you have been
found guilty of, that you
will be spending the rest
of your life in a maximum
security prison with
absolutely no chance of
parole.

THE JUDGE'S CLOSING
REMARK WAS A ---

Now arrange the circled letters to form
the surprise answer, as suggested by the
above cartoon.

Print answer here

JUMBLE®

Unscramble these four Jumbles, one letter to each square, to form four ordinary words.

GERVE

HANTK

LOBWEL

SHELIG

THEIR VIEW OF THE
CARIBBEAN WAS ---

Now arrange the circled letters to form the surprise answer, as suggested by the above cartoon.

Print answer here ◯◯ " ◯◯◯ " ◯◯◯◯◯◯

JUMBLE®

Unscramble these four Jumbles, one letter to each square, to form four ordinary words.

LEECX

LODFO

SIMRYE

BINLEB

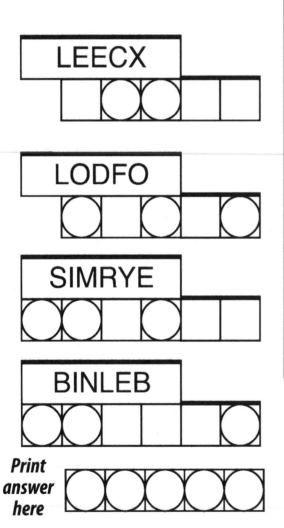

I'm so glad we have a retired handyman like you here in Sun City, Ray.

It's nice to still have odd jobs to do.

THE HANDYMAN AT THE RETIREMENT COMMUNITY LIVED ON A ---

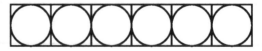

Now arrange the circled letters to form the surprise answer, as suggested by the above cartoon.

Print answer here

152

JUMBLE®

Unscramble these four Jumbles, one letter to each square, to form four ordinary words.

DUENU

GIRRO

PEAQUO

THECKS

Reggie Jackson caught the third out, right there.

Wow! I can't believe this is still alive.

HE WAS ABLE TO TAKE SOME TURF FROM THE OLD YANKEE STADIUM BECAUSE HE WAS THE ----

Now arrange the circled letters to form the surprise answer, as suggested by the above cartoon.

Print answer here

JUMBLE®

Unscramble these four Jumbles, one letter to each square, to form four ordinary words.

GREEV

WORNC

KNITSY

KRUTYE

WELCOME
ELECTRICIANS

I can't wait for the AC/DC modular power supply inventor to speak.

I hear he has a lot of good ideas.

THE ELECTRICIANS
DISCUSSED ---

Now arrange the circled letters to form the surprise answer, as suggested by the above cartoon.

Print answer here

JUMBLE®

Unscramble these four Jumbles, one letter to
each square, to form four ordinary words.

BREEL

DICHE

TCTHIS

GAVYEO

How would you
like to pay for it?

Do you take
credit cards?
I'll get a ton
of airline
miles!

HE USED HIS CREDIT CARD
TO PAY FOR THE ELECTRIC
CAR BECAUSE HE
WANTED TO ----

Now arrange the circled letters to form
the surprise answer, as suggested by the
above cartoon.

Print answer here

JUMBLE®

Unscramble these four Jumbles, one letter to each square, to form four ordinary words.

BEEOS

STUQE

JEBTOC

SUDSIC

Phenomenal Fashions

I can wear this on Halloween. Don't you love it?

Yes, dear.

CASPER AND HIS WIFE SHOPPED IN A ---

Now arrange the circled letters to form the surprise answer, as suggested by the above cartoon.

Print answer here " ◯◯◯ - ◯◯◯◯◯ "

JUMBLE®

Unscramble these four Jumbles, one letter to each square, to form four ordinary words.

PARMC

NUTTS

VERDIR

HOCOYS

We need to have this order to MegaMart by Friday.

I'll call in the third shift and push everyone for overtime.

I hope I can keep up.

AT THE PEANUT BRITTLE FACTORY, IT WAS ----

Now arrange the circled letters to form the surprise answer, as suggested by the above cartoon.

Print answer here

JUMBLE®

Unscramble these four Jumbles, one letter to each square, to form four ordinary words.

HYTEF

DAAWR

FLEMSY

TEPYOR

Looks like we have to make a new plan.

We can take this back road and still get there in time.

DETOUR

SLOW

JUM FAN 1

THEY DIDN'T LET THE DETOUR ---

Now arrange the circled letters to form the surprise answer, as suggested by the above cartoon.

Print answer here

Unscramble these four Jumbles, one letter to
each square, to form four ordinary words.

NEHTT

INGAA

DOIPMU

YIMADS

CITIZEN KANE II

I'm glad I brought
my umbrella.

One for "Citizen
Kane 2."

COMING SOON
Jumble
THE MOVIE

THEY STOOD IN LINE TO
SEE THE MOVIE BECAUSE
THEY HEARD IT WAS ---

Now arrange the circled letters to form
the surprise answer, as suggested by the
above cartoon.

**Print answer
here**

159

JUMBLE®

Unscramble these four Jumbles, one letter to
each square, to form four ordinary words.

ZEDDA

HNIYS

LEPNOL

REZOIC

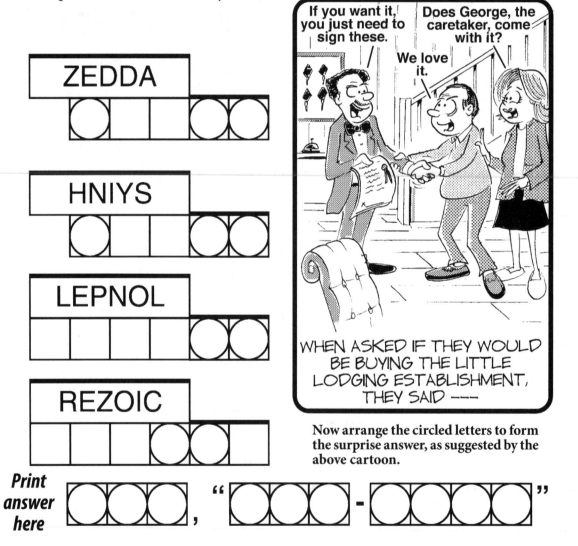

If you want it,
you just need to
sign these.

Does George, the
caretaker, come
with it?

We love
it.

WHEN ASKED IF THEY WOULD
BE BUYING THE LITTLE
LODGING ESTABLISHMENT,
THEY SAID ———

Now arrange the circled letters to form
the surprise answer, as suggested by the
above cartoon.

Print
answer
here

⬜ "⬜ - ⬜"

JUMBLE®

Unscramble these four Jumbles, one letter to each square, to form four ordinary words.

SERSD

DIRNG

NAGRAH

WHORNT

Is this good Champagne?

We only serve the best, ma'am.

Caviar, please.

THE FANCY NEW AIRLINE HAD ---

Now arrange the circled letters to form the surprise answer, as suggested by the above cartoon.

Print answer here

JUMBLE®

Unscramble these four Jumbles, one letter to
each square, to form four ordinary words.

DIRIG

SIHTO

MCONOM

ZAGBOE

I'm all in, old man!

I don't think he's going to beat four of a kind.

I was hoping you'd say that.

FOR THE ROOKIE
POKER PLAYER, WINNING
THE GAME WASN'T ----

Now arrange the circled letters to form
the surprise answer, as suggested by the
above cartoon.

Print
answer
here

JUMBLE®
Kingdom

Challenger
Puzzles

JUMBLE®

Unscramble these six Jumbles, one letter to each square, to form six ordinary words.

GOTUHH

RIREDV

CRABIF

YWLEOL

TOAGUE

GRFODE

Did you get the Jumble today?

THEY WERE ABLE TO STEAL THE PAINTING WHEN THE NIGHT WATCHMAN WAS ---

Now arrange the circled letters to form the surprise answer, as suggested by the above cartoon.

Print answer here

JUMBLE®

Unscramble these six Jumbles, one letter to
each square, to form six ordinary words.

NNTTIE

RAYOMR

ZEEEWH

NMROIF

MINOOT

UVRGLA

You can't keep
doing this!

I'm sorry, sir.
It just keeps
happening.

How does
he keep
his job?

How
does he
keep
his job?

HE WAS LATE FOR HIS
JOB AT THE CLOCK
FACTORY ---

Now arrange the circled letters to form
the surprise answer, as suggested by
the above cartoon.

Print answer here

AND

JUMBLE®

Unscramble these six Jumbles, one letter to each square, to form six ordinary words.

GLEFUN

NNOEAY

DUSEND

VELIYT

OTARUH

RITHME

That was awesome. What a great finale.

THE CONCERT ON THE MOUNTAIN ---

Now arrange the circled letters to form the surprise answer, as suggested by the above cartoon.

Print answer here

ON A

JUMBLE®

Unscramble these six Jumbles, one letter to each square, to form six ordinary words.

PHAREM

TINCUD

SIEYAL

BLINEM

SMIOPE

DINNAL

Isn't that the guy from all those ads?

He's so good-looking!

THE SUCCESSFUL MODEL WAS ABLE TO BUY THE NEW SPORTS CAR BECAUSE HE WAS ––

Now arrange the circled letters to form the surprise answer, as suggested by the above cartoon.

Print answer here

167

JUMBLE®

Unscramble these six Jumbles, one letter to each square, to form six ordinary words.

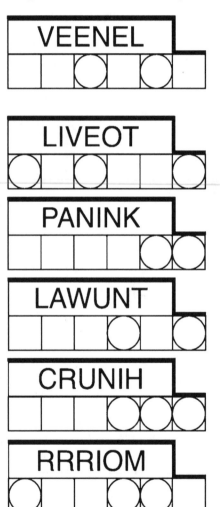

VEENEL

LIVEOT

PANINK

LAWUNT

CRUNIH

RRRIOM

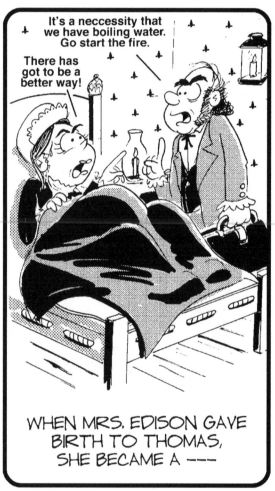

It's a neccessity that we have boiling water. Go start the fire.

There has got to be a better way!

WHEN MRS. EDISON GAVE BIRTH TO THOMAS, SHE BECAME A ---

Now arrange the circled letters to form the surprise answer, as suggested by the above cartoon.

Print answer here

OF

JUMBLE

Unscramble these six Jumbles, one letter to each square, to form six ordinary words.

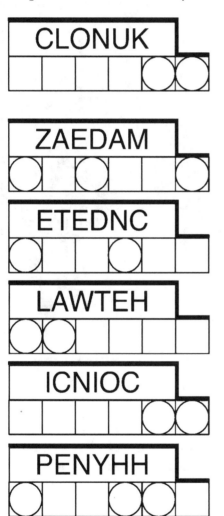

CLONUK

ZAEDAM

ETEDNC

LAWTEH

ICNIOC

PENYHH

What a long day. I need to lie down and take it easy for a while.

Here, you look dehydrated.

AFTER A LONG DAY OF CASTING SPELLS AND WREAKING HAVOC, THE EVIL WITCH HAD A ----

Now arrange the circled letters to form the surprise answer, as suggested by the above cartoon.

Print answer here

JUMBLE.

Unscramble these six Jumbles, one letter to each square, to form six ordinary words.

TESTEL

HNUKRS

MUMIEN

ROTDIR

KYNCAR

CASUCE

I'm telling you for the last time. I have white stripes.

Oh, my.

They're black!

THE GIRAFFE WAS GOING TO TRY TO BREAK UP THE FIGHT BETWEEN THE ZEBRAS, BUT DECIDED NOT TO ----

Now arrange the circled letters to form the surprise answer, as suggested by the above cartoon.

Print answer here

JUMBLE®

Unscramble these six Jumbles, one letter to each square, to form six ordinary words.

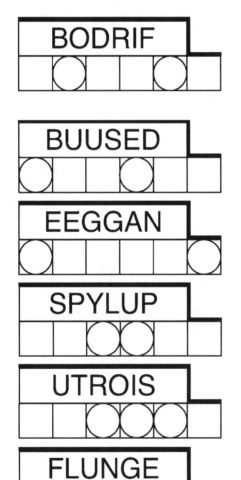

BODRIF

BUUSED

EEGGAN

SPYLUP

UTROIS

FLUNGE

I'm tired of flying solo. Will you marry me?

This must be the premiere of that new series they keep running commercials about.

I doubt this show is going to last.

THE NEW TV SHOW ABOUT THE AVIATORS WAS THIS.

Now arrange the circled letters to form the surprise answer, as suggested by the above cartoon.

Print answer here

A

JUMBLE®

Unscramble these six Jumbles, one letter to
each square, to form six ordinary words.

SHOCOY

SALVIH

UWATOL

NACCEH

SSMYTE

CITPED

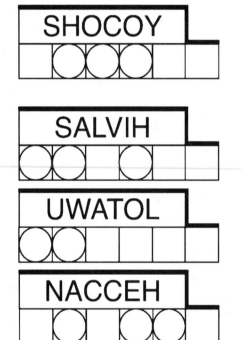

THE HUNGRY HEIFER

What with all the overtime at
work, my bowling league,
golfing and my weekly
poker game, I just don't
have the time to go to the
gym.

When are you
going to start
using your gym
membership?

HE WANTED TO START
GOING TO THE GYM
REGULARLY, BUT
HE HAD ----

Now arrange the circled letters to form
the surprise answer, as suggested by
the above cartoon.

Print answer here

JUMBLE®

Unscramble these six Jumbles, one letter to each square, to form six ordinary words.

DOMETS

HIDARS

YLIPMS

HILANE

YOUFLJ

NISSIT

When I was little, we were taught that our solar system had nine planets.

Were there people living on Mars then, too?

CALLING PLUTO A PLANET WILL BECOME A ---

Now arrange the circled letters to form the surprise answer, as suggested by the above cartoon.

Print answer here

JUMBLE®

Unscramble these six Jumbles, one letter to
each square, to form six ordinary words.

ZENLOZ

OXSEPE

NESCOH

TUAPED

FUWORR

TRETOX

I may flutter like a
bat, but how do
you like that,
Frankie?

One, two, three...

HE WAS THIS WHEN HE
LOST THE BOXING MATCH
TO DRACULA.

Now arrange the circled letters to form
the surprise answer, as suggested by
the above cartoon.

Print answer here

JUMBLE®

Unscramble these six Jumbles, one letter to each square, to form six ordinary words.

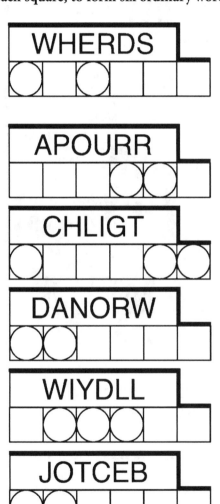

WHERDS

APOURR

CHLIGT

DANORW

WIYDLL

JOTCEB

Now, line it up with the studs and put nails 16 inches apart.

WHERE THE CARPENTERS LEARNED THEIR TRADE.

Now arrange the circled letters to form the surprise answer, as suggested by the above cartoon.

Print answer here

JUMBLE®

Unscramble these six Jumbles, one letter to each square, to form six ordinary words.

PGURMY

YAGNEC

THIGLC

KAANEW

TATNUR

OEEPUT

If you're ticklish, that means you like Cameron. Look! You're ticklish.

Stop tickling me...I'm serious!!!

TO HER, BEING TICKLED BY HER BIG SISTER WAS ----

Now arrange the circled letters to form the surprise answer, as suggested by the above cartoon.

Print answer here

JUMBLE®

Unscramble these six Jumbles, one letter to each square, to form six ordinary words.

ROMETH

LOTUND

LEFNAL

DOTLED

CECINS

HATURO

Hey! What are you doing? We're going to miss the plane!

Just a second. I almost passed this up.

AFTER SPOTTING THE LOOSE CHANGE ON THE GROUND, HE ----

Now arrange the circled letters to form the surprise answer, as suggested by the above cartoon.

Print answer here

JUMBLE®

Unscramble these six Jumbles, one letter to
each square, to form six ordinary words.

DIRALA

DEHNID

HOLYUR

EXLUDE

ASETTT

VELYIT

I guess I'll
take it. But
are you sure
you don't
have any
live human
parts?

Take it or leave
it. Report to
makeup.

HE TOOK THE ROLE
AS A ZOMBIE, BUT HE
WASN'T ———

Now arrange the circled letters to form
the surprise answer, as suggested by
the above cartoon.

Print answer here

JUMBLE®

Unscramble these six Jumbles, one letter to each square, to form six ordinary words.

MOVULE

SHHART

LEGFUN

KANHES

LISAYE

ROLALD

SHE WAS ANXIOUS TO START THE RIDING LESSON, BUT THE INSTRUCTOR WANTED THE STUDENT TO - - -

Now arrange the circled letters to form the surprise answer, as suggested by the above cartoon.

Print answer here

JUMBLE®

Unscramble these six Jumbles, one letter to each square, to form six ordinary words.

TIONNO

NOFLYD

SMIRPH

WRROBO

TEPLOP

HERBUC

The bisque sounds good, but $24 is way too much.

You need a salad. Your doctor told you to watch your cholesterol.

HE DIDN'T ORDER THE LOBSTER BISQUE BECAUSE IT WAS---

Now arrange the circled letters to form the surprise answer, as suggested by the above cartoon.

Print answer here

JUMBLE®

Unscramble these six Jumbles, one letter to each square, to form six ordinary words.

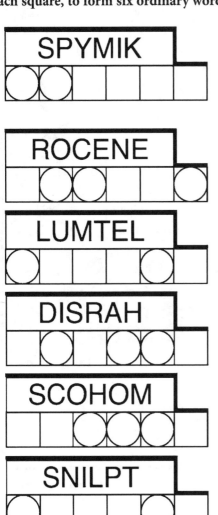

SPYMIK

ROCENE

LUMTEL

DISRAH

SCOHOM

SNILPT

All right. But I'm keeping all tips.

I told you. We need a 20% bigger cut for you to work the games.

IF HE WANTED TO GET A NEW CONTRACT TO SELL SODAS AND HOT DOGS AT THE STADIUM, HE WOULD NEED TO ----

Now arrange the circled letters to form the surprise answer, as suggested by the above cartoon.

Print answer here

JUMBLE

Unscramble these six Jumbles, one letter to
each square, to form six ordinary words.

ROTTHA

TENNIY

YEGRES

MIFRLY

REVFIY

RATNOY

Hey! Can
someone get me
a blood pressure
cuff?

I've been
telling him
to take it
easy.

We're going
to run some
more tests.

THE PATIENT IN THE
BUSY HOSPITAL
ROOM LONGED
FOR THE – – –

Now arrange the circled letters to form
the surprise answer, as suggested by
the above cartoon.

Print answer here

JUMBLE®

Unscramble these six Jumbles, one letter to each square, to form six ordinary words.

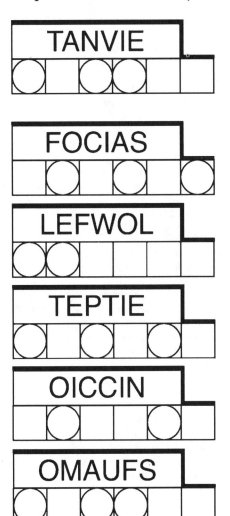

TANVIE

FOCIAS

LEFWOL

TEPTIE

OICCIN

OMAUFS

Come on in! I'll stuff that for next to nothing.

WE'LL BEAT ANYONE'S PRICES!

How can I take this guy on?

THE NEW TAXIDERMIST MOVING TO TOWN GAVE THE OLD TAXIDERMIST ---

Now arrange the circled letters to form the surprise answer, as suggested by the above cartoon.

Print answer here

Answers

1. **Jumbles:** VOCAL SORRY METRIC TRIPLE
   Answer: Getting a cardio workout by dancing to disco made them—RETRO-ACTIVE

2. **Jumbles:** EXERT WHISK UPROAR GUILTY
   Answer: They would have been better off if the boat had more of these—EXIT ROWS

3. **Jumbles:** CYNIC THINK EXEMPT FOSSIL
   Answer: The retired hockey player lived here—IN THE STICKS

4. **Jumbles:** GRAPH STRUM TODDLE EXCEED
   Answer: When she asked him if he wanted a small amount of coffee, he said he wanted—A LATTE

5. **Jumbles:** HONEY KIOSK SYMBOL CRAFTY
   Answer: What they called the bad Irish tribute band—SHAM ROCK

6. **Jumbles:** PURGE PANIC THRIVE RADISH
   Answer: After winning the big hand, he was this—CHIPPER

7. **Jumbles:** RELIC HYENA MUTATE BIGGER
   Answer: He was able to start his traffic signal business after his banker gave him this—THE GREEN LIGHT

8. **Jumbles:** INEPT UNITY DIFFER AGENDA
   Answer: When the health inspector found a fly in his lobster bisque, it resulted in this—FINE DINING

9. **Jumbles:** BISON MERCY ONWARD NOODLE
   Answer: After seeing how wrinkled his suit was, Superman would become this—IRON MAN

10. **Jumbles:** BATCH KHAKI FABRIC EXHALE
    Answer: When the state park levied a usage fee for its trails, he faced a—TAX HIKE

11. **Jumbles:** SNUCK BEACH ACROSS DOUBLE
    Answer: After their defeat the night before, the coach wanted his team to do this—BOUNCE BACK

12. **Jumbles:** TRACK MORPH INFUSE DIVINE
    Answer: While the men were away, the women—MANNED THE FORT

13. **Jumbles:** FOCAL ELECT INFANT BEWARE
    Answer: When he talked to himself in the mirror, he talked to himself—FACE-"TWO"-FACE

14. **Jumbles:** BLUFF GECKO EXOTIC IMPOSE
    Answer: They teed off in Cancun to experience the—"GOLF" OF MEXICO

15. **Jumbles:** HOUSE TIPSY SALMON WISDOM
    Answer: Getting fired was this to the anchorman—NEWS TO HIM

16. **Jumbles:** AFTER NOTCH ACCENT JAGUAR
    Answer: When it came to her husband's plan to successfully lose weight, she thought he had this—A FAT CHANCE

17. **Jumbles:** DOUGH SQUAB USEFUL ASYLUM
    Answer: After a long day of planting hedges, she was this—BUSHED

18. **Jumbles:** GLOAT DRESS COTTON PURIFY
    Answer: The designs for the new eyeglasses were chosen after this—FOCUS TESTING

19. **Jumbles:** TROLL TREND WEIGHT VALLEY
    Answer: He was bummed after failing to clear the hurdle, but he would—GET OVER IT

20. **Jumbles:** VENOM ADOPT COBWEB PRANCE
    Answer: His chef's award-winning pizza was so good that it couldn't—BE TOPPED

21. **Jumbles:** EDGED FANCY PLACID GENTRY
    Answer: The submarine needed a—DEEP CLEANING

22. **Jumbles:** WHIRL MUSTY COBALT ABACUS
    Answer: The gun wouldn't fire because—IT WAS SHOT

23. **Jumbles:** GRIME TWINE BESTOW WHIMSY
    Answer: Looking for the perfect new outfit can be—A TRYING TIME

24. **Jumbles:** PRESS CLASH TUNEUP EXPERT
    Answer: When the baby wouldn't sleep, the parents got—LESS REST

25. **Jumbles:** DOZED NACHO AFFECT DRIVER
    Answer: The politician spoke frankly to his dinner companion because he was a—CANDID DATE

26. **Jumbles:** UNITY SOUPY PURPLE REVERT
    Answer: Taking a nap on the summit allowed the mountain climber to—REST UP

27. **Jumbles:** AMAZE STUNG SPIRAL POSTAL
    Answer: When it came time to decide on a starting quarterback, the coach was—AT AN IMPASSE

28. **Jumbles:** OPERA VODKA UNWIND STRING
    Answer: The crocodile's cousin was a—NAVIGATOR

29. **Jumbles:** DOUSE GROUP ENGINE ROOKIE
    Answer: The supermodel twins showed off their—GOOD GENES

30. **Jumbles:** SPELL RATIO POUNCE GROOVY
    Answer: An important way to compensate our veterans is to—PAY RESPECT

31. **Jumbles:** REBEL GLOAT LIZARD SPLASH
    Answer: When King Kong agreed to buy the Empire State Building, it was a—BIG DEAL

32. **Jumbles:** AWFUL WHEEL BULLET MOTION
    Answer: He was able to recover the fumble because he was—ON THE BALL

33. **Jumbles:** AGENT MOUND SAILOR AFLAME
    Answer: Finding sneakers for some basketball players is—NO SMALL FEAT

34. **Jumbles:** ODDLY PRONG ACCUSE ABRUPT
    Answer: The nursery owner told her new employee the—GROUND RULES

35. **Jumbles:** INEPT SKULL BREACH ANYONE
    Answer: Buffalo's NFL team hired an accountant to do this—PAY THE BILLS

36. **Jumbles:** WEARY ORBIT WEAPON DETACH
    Answer: Mozart's achievements were—NOTEWORTHY

37. **Jumbles:** DOUSE VIGIL FROZEN WALLOP
    Answer: At one time, reading a book on a Nook, Kindle or iPad was a—NOVEL IDEA

38. **Jumbles:** CROAK VENOM DREDGE KITTEN
    Answer: The zombie boxer's manager told him to—KNOCK 'EM DEAD

39. **Jumbles:** WAFER OBESE MONKEY GUTTER
    Answer: Barry Manilow didn't want to forget his idea for a new song, so he—WROTE A NOTE

40. **Jumbles:** BLISS NINTH REGRET NOVICE
    Answer: The scout outing was—"IN-TENTS"

41. **Jumbles:** TENTH AUDIO CRUNCH HAMMER
    Answer: Leaves falling off the trees each year is—"AUTUMN-MATIC"

42. **Jumbles:** BRAWN HEDGE DISOWN RITUAL
    Answer: The fancy new pub really—RAISED THE BAR

43. **Jumbles:** SIGHT DERBY SCULPT MEMORY
    Answer: When they asked the owner of the inn if they could check in early, he said—BE MY GUEST

44. **Jumbles:** UPPER TRUNK ANNUAL CHANGE
    Answer: The Jumble artist refused to draw the cartoon because he thought the wordplay was—"PUN-GENT"

45. **Jumbles:** PLUMB PLUCK DEARLY TIMBER
    Answer: Everything was going great on her European vacation until she—TRIPPED

46. **Jumbles:** SCUFF THUMP TICKET AFFORD
    Answer: The limo driver had been working for years but he didn't have much to—"CHAUFFEUR" IT

47. **Jumbles:** FOYER RAYON FACTOR FLIGHT
    Answer: The new shoe store was doing quite well thanks to all the—FOOT TRAFFIC

48. **Jumbles:** RIGOR MINCE EXPAND HUMBLE
    Answer: After forgetting to pay his gym dues, he needed to—"RE-MEMBER"

49. **Jumbles:** CARGO TRACT PULPIT ATRIUM
    Answer: When the prisoner was shipped off to Alcatraz, he went on a—GUILT TRIP

50. **Jumbles:** ELDER ELECT WALRUS TOPPED
    Answer: It was quiet on the submarine because most of the crew was in—A DEEP SLEEP

51. **Jumbles:** PANTS PURGE BANISH DEPICT
    Answer: After the rope broke, he—SNAPPED

52. **Jumbles:** LUNCH ADAPT NARROW POLICE
    Answer: He tried to teach his son how to fish, but his son couldn't—CATCH ON

53. **Jumbles:** BLIMP INEPT THORAX PALLET
    Answer: He wanted to buy the classic drum set, but someone—BEAT HIM TO IT

54. **Jumbles:** BRISK VAULT REDUCE PARLAY
    Answer: When the actress started appearing in commercials, she became a—"SELL-EBRITY"

55. **Jumbles:** STUNK ETHIC ALPACA AWAKEN
    Answer: She mistakenly thought that owning a bakery would be a—CAKE WALK

56. **Jumbles:** DWARF TABOO TRENDY DISCUS
    Answer: Installing the new fan at the gym was—NO SWEAT

57. **Jumbles:** PRIOR OFTEN WALNUT ACCESS
    Answer: Death Valley is so hot thanks in part to its—"LOW-CATION"

58. **Jumbles:** HOIST NEEDY APIECE QUEASY
    Answer: If the Jumble makers' play on words isn't good enough, they might get—"PUN-ISHED" (not really)

59. **Jumbles:** WEARY MILKY HUDDLE PLURAL
    Answer: The pitcher's son loved it when his father—WALKED HIM

60. **Jumbles:** FETCH EXERT POLICY BEAUTY
    Answer: After his wife struck it big on a slot machine, he was happy to have a—"BETTOR" HALF

61. **Jumbles:** JOKER TOKEN BITTEN AVENUE
    Answer: When they discussed creating a company to make artificial knees, they planned a—JOINT VENTURE

62. **Jumbles:** ANNEX DRESS APATHY OBLIGE
    Answer: After seeing her former husband for the first time in years, she was not—"EX-SIGHTED"

63. **Jumbles:** AWARD IMAGE DRENCH POORLY
    Answer: The cartooning competition would end—IN A DRAW

64. **Jumbles:** FRONT SWEPT FICKLE RATHER
    Answer: The author's expenses related to doing research for a new book would be—WRITTEN OFF

65. **Jumbles:** GOOSE NEEDY SCULPT WINDOW
    Answer: They studied up on Death Valley before their trip there so that they could get the—LOWDOWN

66. **Jumbles:** SNIFF THIRD UNTOLD INTENT
    Answer: When Mickey Mantle made his debut with the NY Yankees on 4-17-1951, he did this with his new teammates—HIT IT OFF

67. **Jumbles:** GRAND FROND SCENIC FEWEST
    Answer: Tensions mounted between the lemonade sellers when neither of them would—STAND DOWN

68. **Jumbles:** DUNCE TROLL ABRUPT ABACUS
    Answer: When he proposed that there were oceans on the moon, some people thought it was—"LUNA-SEA"

69. **Jumbles:** BLAZE POUCH SIMILE ROTARY
    Answer: Everyone thought her new wig was—"HAIR-LARIOUS"

70. **Jumbles:** GIANT ARRAY FORMAL MARSHY
    Answer: The "garden" was always in "danger" because it was—AN ANAGRAM

71. **Jumbles:** EPOXY NEEDY MATRIX IDIOCY
    Answer: Everything was going fine as he chopped down the tree until the—"AXE-IDENT"

72. **Jumbles:** DIGIT STRUM CASING POUNCE
    Answer: The owner of the rug store had—CAR PETS

73. **Jumbles:** SHOVE BLAND HIDDEN FIDDLE
    Answer: He didn't make a very good archaeologist because he was a—BONEHEAD

74. **Jumbles:** AWAKE HURRY DEPICT OUTING
    Answer: When all the cartoonists gathered for the weekend they were—DRAWN TOGETHER

75. **Jumbles:** VERGE ROBIN REVERT FABRIC
    Answer: Congress designated that Memorial Day would always be the last Monday in May so that we'd—NEVER FORGET

76. **Jumbles:** STAND BLOOM RABBIT VISION
    Answer: Everything was fine at the amphibian bar until the frog sat on the—TOAD'S STOOL

77. **Jumbles:** SLANT TOXIC STOOGE AFLOAT
    Answer: The U.S. geography teacher wanted the student to—STATE FACTS

78. **Jumbles:** PINCH BUDDY BRUNCH EFFORT
    Answer: The food at the restaurant was so bad that customers were getting—FED UP

79. **Jumbles:** DOUSE APART OUTING EXPERT
    Answer: He became one after telling his wife how to drive—A PEDESTRIAN

80. **Jumbles:** OCTET PRESS BAKERY THRIVE
    Answer: When the identical twins built the staircase, they became—STEP BROTHERS

81. **Jumbles:** VODKA EAGLE SAILOR IMPORT
    Answer: The mix-up at the cemetery was a—GRAVE MISTAKE

82. **Jumbles:** OFTEN AWARE MOSAIC MOTION
    Answer: Bill Gates bought the new cashmere robe because he wanted to upgrade his—"SOFTWEAR"

83. **Jumbles:** BOTCH YOUTH KETTLE SEPTIC
    Answer: When he asked, "Should we harvest the strawberries or the blueberries?" she said—YOU PICK

84. **Jumbles:** ANKLE TOXIC VULGAR THIRST
    Answer: The crocodile needed help solving a case, so she called in—AN "INVESTI-GATOR"

85. **Jumbles:** IDIOT GLOAT HERMIT BOTANY
    Answer: The lobster was this at the prospect of becoming someone's dinner—BOILING MAD

86. **Jumbles:** OPERA HEFTY BOUNCE CAMPUS
    Answer: The baseball player bought a treadmill for—HOME RUNS

87. **Jumbles:** INEPT MIGHT LENGTH TIRADE
    Answer: He didn't believe in the inventor's plans for the incandescent bulb, so Edison—ENLIGHTENED HIM

88. **Jumbles:** TACKY AUDIO FLAWED GOALIE
    Answer: When the Red Sox took a huge lead, the fans at Fenway Park had a—FIELD DAY

89. **Jumbles:** AXIOM BLURT FEEBLE OUTLET
    Answer: When it came to scheduling her next gymnastics lesson, the student was—FLEXIBLE

90. **Jumbles:** ALPHA TRUNK PERSON FEMALE
    Answer: After the buffet aboard the cruise ship, everyone came to a—FULL STOP

91. **Jumbles:** SPOIL ADULT SPRAWL TURNIP
Answer: When he finally had a chance to go around the slow car, he couldn't—PASS IT UP

92. **Jumbles:** CRACK KAYAK UPROOT USEFUL
Answer: The 4th of July caused sales at the fireworks store to—SKYROCKET

93. **Jumbles:** KIOSK LIGHT UPBEAT ENTICE
Answer: After he retired, King Arthur opened a—"KNIGHT" CLUB

94. **Jumbles:** ODDLY FAULT INVEST ISLAND
Answer: No matter how hard he tried, he just couldn't keep his boat-building business—AFLOAT

95. **Jumbles:** HELIX SCOUT MIGHTY AZALEA
Answer: The soccer match in Bangkok was—A "THAI" GAME

96. **Jumbles:** SCOUR HATCH IODINE SCARCE
Answer: The baseball team's pitching instructor lived in—A COACH HOUSE

97. **Jumbles:** METAL CLOAK ADVENT BILLOW
Answer: Lassie was a bit depressed and feeling—"MELAN-COLLIE"

98. **Jumbles:** LOFTY SWUNG INDUCE HYPHEN
Answer: Porky applied for a job as an airline pilot, but the airline said—WHEN PIGS FLY

99. **Jumbles:** ABOUT SAUTE ASTHMA CLEVER
Answer: The teenager constantly oversleeping was—CAUSE FOR ALARM

100. **Jumbles:** ELDER LARVA VACANT WHIMSY
Answer: The ironworkers listened to—HEAVY METAL

101. **Jumbles:** QUIRK PLUME SOCIAL WORTHY
Answer: Compared to the competition, the losing poker player didn't—STACK UP

102. **Jumbles:** GROVE ENJOY LIVING BUMMER
Answer: Where Tarzan worked out—AT THE JUNGLE GYM

103. **Jumbles:** BUNCH CARAT LOADED FAIRLY
Answer: Thanks to the fender-bender, she met her future husband—BY ACCIDENT

104. **Jumbles:** CHOKE DAISY SLEEPY FATHER
Answer: Even though it was plugged in, the electric guitar without strings was—"CHORD-LESS"

105. **Jumbles:** SHINY BRIBE SPLINT INFANT
Answer: The newborn fish slept in a—"BASS-IN-NET"

106. **Jumbles:** ADOPT DROOP PERSON SPRUCE
Answer: The four-star general hated following the—DOCTOR'S ORDERS

107. **Jumbles:** SUSHI HUMID SLEIGH ODDEST
Answer: A student had the idea that they should get out of school early, but the teacher—DISMISSED IT

108. **Jumbles:** SORRY BRAVO BICKER PERMIT
Answer: He was struggling to find a new guitar because he was—TOO PICKY

109. **Jumbles:** TIPSY PILOT DRESSY FIERCE
Answer: When it came to building the new staircase, getting plans drawn up was—THE FIRST STEP

110. **Jumbles:** FINCH DITTO WHEEZE MENACE
Answer: The guys at the pig roast—CHEWED THE FAT

111. **Jumbles:** PANIC TRACK JOVIAL BEMUSE
Answer: The Australian rancher was building his new barn—OUT BACK

112. **Jumbles:** REBEL STASH PARADE PIGLET
Answer: The weightlifter's new world record—RAISED THE BAR

113. **Jumbles:** PIANO ELUDE BALLAD ANYHOW
Answer: When the first settlers saw the Grand Canyon, they said—"LOW" AND BEHOLD

114. **Jumbles:** LEMUR FORGO CASINO PANTRY
Answer: The flower shop owner had a side job as a—"FLOORIST"

115. **Jumbles:** AWAKE FORCE WARMLY ZENITH
Answer: The rooster meteorologist predicted—"FOWL" WEATHER

116. **Jumbles:** PLUSH PIXEL FATHOM WRITER
Answer: His father wanted him to become a tailor, but the prospect didn't—SUIT HIM

117. **Jumbles:** MUDDY MINUS ROTATE BANDIT
Answer: When the U.S. government decided to expand coin production to Denver, they—MADE A MINT

118. **Jumbles:** FANCY RUGBY SETTLE BALLET
Answer: The tower in Paris was an—EYEFUL

119. **Jumbles:** ADMIT CHAOS ROOKIE RUDDER
Answer: The man who wasn't as wealthy as he led people to believe was—DISCREDITED

120. **Jumbles:** ROYAL ENACT CHANGE SCRIPT
Answer: The pony with the negative attitude was—A "NEIGH-SAYER"

121. **Jumbles:** TRICK GUARD INVOKE EYELID
Answer: The man who sold fake tennis equipment online was charged with—RACKETEERING

122. **Jumbles:** DWELL HILLY FAMOUS BREACH
Answer: The contractor wanted to pay this for his tree purchases—"HOLE-SALE"

123. **Jumbles:** RODEO BRISK ICONIC PIRACY
Answer: His tour of Alcatraz turned into this when he fell down the stairs—PRISON BREAK

124. **Jumbles:** OMEGA TRICK ACQUIT HANGAR
Answer: The cooks at the new breakfast restaurant were ready to—GET CRACKING

125. **Jumbles:** MINCE HOBBY LAVISH ABSURD
Answer: When the young sheep fought over their sleeping arrangements, it was—"BED-LAMB"

126. **Jumbles:** CHORD STOOD AFFIRM TOWARD
Answer: When he ate dinner in his new recliner, he ate—COMFORT FOOD

127. **Jumbles:** OMEGA HOLLY SEASON ADRIFT
Answer: The pirate was ready to retire because he was—ON HIS LAST LEG

128. **Jumbles:** PUPIL ABOVE AUBURN UNLOCK
Answer: The hot-air balloon sank after they ran out of fuel, but he had a—BACK-UP PLAN

129. **Jumbles:** CHOMP UNITY GLITCH FALTER
Answer: After walking through the smokers to get inside, she was—FUMING

130. **Jumbles:** PLUMP SEEDY SHRUNK AGENDA
Answer: The ice cream parlor's weekly newsletter was the—"SUNDAE" PAPER

131. **Jumbles:** HARSH BRAVO SEASON FACTOR
Answer: After seeing his identical twin's new look, he said—OH, BROTHER

132. **Jumbles:** AGILE ODDLY INCOME DIVERT
Answer: At the height of his singing career, Jim Morrison was—"A-DOOR-ED"

133. **Jumbles:** THANK GAUGE SICKEN WINNER
Answer: This section of the gym was a—"WEIGHTING" AREA

134. **Jumbles:** TOXIN DECAY CHURCH BECKON
Answer: She was going to try the spicy hot wings, but she—CHICKENED OUT

135. **Jumbles:** PUNCH DINKY PONCHO BEAVER
Answer: The arm wrestler was about to win because he had the—UPPER HAND

136. **Jumbles:** PYLON MOLDY PILLAR MISUSE
Answer: The Cyclops teacher had just—ONE PUPIL

137. **Jumbles:** HOIST MERGE GALAXY FUSION
Answer: Porky had to leave the basketball game after he injured his—HAMSTRING

138. **Jumbles:** HABIT GUEST POTENT MEDLEY
Answer: They watched the sun go down from the beach because it was a perfect—SETTING

139. **Jumbles:** ENACT FILMY STEREO FIBULA
Answer: His father's neckwear collection was full of—FAMILY TIES

140. **Jumbles:** PRONE THIRD RADISH BAFFLE
Answer: Feeding the hawks, vultures and owls at the zoo was sometimes—FOR THE BIRDS

141. **Jumbles:** STYLE VISOR IMMUNE GAMING
Answer: Lunchtime at the prison was—SERVING TIME

142. **Jumbles:** POISE DODGE PANTRY SHRINK
Answer: Hoping to fill the seat of the disgraced councilman, he was—DIS-APPOINTED

143. **Jumbles:** SWUNG DAISY EVOLVE SYSTEM
Answer: The special pricing at the bakery was a—SWEET DEAL

144. **Jumbles:** OPERA NINTH SUPERB FACADE
Answer: After a long day working at the cemetery, the groundskeeper wished he could—REST IN PEACE

145. **Jumbles:** ETHIC MERGE KITTEN NOTARY
Answer: The tourists were confused in Athens because everything was—GREEK TO THEM

146. **Jumbles:** APART DODGE FONDLY CURFEW
Answer: The animals in the forest got along so well because they were all—GOOD-NATURED

147. **Jumbles:** UNFIT BAGGY UNPAID IDIOCY
Answer: The street vendor told her it was an authentic handbag, but she wasn't—BUYING IT

148. **Jumbles:** SPELL TOXIN ENCORE GLANCE
Answer: The judge's closing remark was a—LONG SENTENCE

149. **Jumbles:** VERGE THANK BELLOW SLEIGH
Answer: Their view of the Caribbean was—AT "SEE" LEVEL

150. **Jumbles:** EXCEL FLOOD MISERY NIBBLE
Answer: The handyman at the retirement community lived on a—FIXED INCOME

151. **Jumbles:** UNDUE RIGOR OPAQUE SKETCH
Answer: He was able to take some turf from the old Yankee stadium because he was the—GROUNDSKEEPER

152. **Jumbles:** VERGE CROWN STINKY TURKEY
Answer: The electricians discussed—CURRENT EVENTS

153. **Jumbles:** REBEL CHIDE STITCH VOYAGE
Answer: He used his credit card to pay for the electric car because he wanted to—CHARGE IT

154. **Jumbles:** OBESE QUEST OBJECT DISCUS
Answer: Casper and his wife shopped in a—"BOO-TIQUE"

155. **Jumbles:** CRAMP STUNT DRIVER CHOOSY
Answer: At the peanut brittle factory it was—CRUNCH TIME

156. **Jumbles:** HEFTY AWARD MYSELF POETRY
Answer: They didn't let the detour—DETER THEM

157. **Jumbles:** TENTH AGAIN PODIUM DISMAY
Answer: They stood in line to see the movie because they heard it was—OUTSTANDING

158. **Jumbles:** DAZED SHINY POLLEN COZIER
Answer: When asked if they would be buying the little lodging establishment, they said—YES, "INN-DEED"

159. **Jumbles:** DRESS GRIND HANGAR THROWN
Answer: The fancy new airline had—HIGH STANDARDS

160. **Jumbles:** RIGID HOIST COMMON GAZEBO
Answer: For the rookie poker player, winning the game wasn't—IN THE CARDS

161. **Jumbles:** THOUGH FABRIC OUTAGE DRIVER YELLOW FORGED
Answer: They were able to steal the painting when the night watchman was—CAUGHT OFF-GUARD

162. **Jumbles:** INTENT WHEEZE MOTION ARMORY INFORM VULGAR
Answer: He was late for his job at the clock factory—TIME AND TIME AGAIN

163. **Jumbles:** ENGULF SUDDEN AUTHOR ANYONE LEVITY HERMIT
Answer: The concert on the mountain—ENDED ON A HIGH NOTE

164. **Jumbles:** HAMPER EASILY IMPOSE INDUCT NIMBLE INLAND
Answer: The successful male model was able to buy the new sports car because he was—PAID HANDSOMELY

165. **Jumbles:** ELEVEN NAPKIN URCHIN VIOLET WALNUT MIRROR
Answer: When Mrs. Edison gave birth to Thomas, she became a—MOTHER OF INVENTION

166. **Jumbles:** UNLOCK DECENT ICONIC AMAZED WEALTH HYPHEN
Answer: After a long day of casting spells and wreaking havoc, the evil witch had a—WICKED HEADACHE

167. **Jumbles:** SETTLE IMMUNE CRANKY SHRUNK TORRID ACCUSE
Answer: The giraffe was going to try to break up the fight between the zebras, but decided not to—STICK HIS NECK OUT

168. **Jumbles:** FORBID ENGAGE SUITOR SUBDUE SUPPLY ENGULF
Answer: The new TV show about the aviators was this—A PILOT EPISODE

169. **Jumbles:** CHOOSY OUTLAW SYSTEM LAVISH CHANCE DEPICT
Answer: He wanted to start going to the gym regularly, but he had—TOO MUCH ON HIS PLATE

170. **Jumbles:** MODEST SIMPLY JOYFUL RADISH INHALE INSIST
Answer: Calling Pluto a planet will become a—DISTANT MEMORY

171. **Jumbles:** NOZZLE CHOSEN FURROW EXPOSE UPDATE EXTORT
Answer: He was this when he lost the boxing match to Dracula—DOWN FOR THE COUNT

172. **Jumbles:** SHREWD GLITCH WILDLY UPROAR ONWARD OBJECT
Answer: Where the carpenters learned their trade—BOARDING SCHOOL

173. **Jumbles:** GRUMPY GLITCH TRUANT AGENCY AWAKEN TOUPEE
Answer: To her, being tickled by her big sister was—NO LAUGHING MATTER

174. **Jumbles:** MOTHER FALLEN SCENIC UNTOLD TODDLE AUTHOR
Answer: After spotting the loose change on the ground, he—TURNED ON A DIME

175. **Jumbles:** RADIAL HOURLY ATTEST HIDDEN DELUXE LEVITY
Answer: He took the role as a zombie, but he wasn't—THRILLED TO DEATH

176. **Jumbles:** VOLUME ENGULF EASILY THRASH SHAKEN DOLLAR
Answer: She was anxious to start the riding lesson, but the instructor wanted the student to—HOLD HER HORSES

177. **Jumbles:** NOTION SHRIMP TOPPLE FONDLY BORROW CHERUB
Answer: He didn't order the lobster bisque because it was—TOO RICH FOR HIS BLOOD

178. **Jumbles:** SKIMPY MULLET SMOOCH ENCORE RADISH SPLINT
Answer: If he wanted to get a new contract to sell sodas and hot dogs at the stadium, he would need to—MAKE CONCESSIONS

179. **Jumbles:** THROAT GEYSER VERIFY NINETY FIRMLY NOTARY
Answer: The patient in the busy hospital room longed for the—SILENT TREATMENT

180. **Jumbles:** NATIVE FELLOW ICONIC FIASCO PETITE FAMOUS
Answer: The new taxidermist moving to town gave the old taxidermist—STIFF COMPETITION

Need More Jumbles®?

Jumble® Books

More than 175 puzzles each!

Jammin' Jumble®
$9.95 • ISBN: 1-57243-844-4

Java Jumble®
$9.95 • ISBN: 978-1-60078-415-6

Jazzy Jumble®
$9.95 • ISBN: 978-1-57243-962-7

Jet Set Jumble®
$9.95 • ISBN: 978-1-60078-353-1

Joyful Jumble®
$9.95 • ISBN: 978-1-60078-079-0

Juke Joint Jumble®
$9.95 • ISBN: 978-1-60078-295-4

Jumble® at Work
$9.95 • ISBN: 1-57243-147-4

Jumble® Celebration
$9.95 • ISBN: 978-1-60078-134-6

Jumble® Circus
$9.95 • ISBN: 978-1-60078-739-3

Jumble® Exploer
$9.95 • ISBN: 978-1-60078-854-3

Jumble® Explosion
$9.95 • ISBN: 978-1-60078-078-3

Jumble® Fever
$9.95 • ISBN: 1-57243-593-3

Jumble® Fiesta
$9.95 • ISBN: 1-57243-626-3

Jumble® Fun
$9.95 • ISBN: 1-57243-379-5

Jumble® Galaxy
$9.95 • ISBN: 978-1-60078-583-2

Jumble® Genius
$9.95 • ISBN: 1-57243-896-7

Jumble® Getaway
$9.95 • ISBN: 978-1-60078-547-4

Jumble® Grab Bag
$9.95 • ISBN: 1-57243-273-X

Jumble® Jackpot
$9.95 • ISBN: 1-57243-897-5

Jumble® Jailbreak
$9.95 • ISBN: 978-1-62937-002-6

Jumble® Jambalaya
$9.95 • ISBN: 978-1-60078-294-7

Jumble® Jamboree
$9.95 • ISBN: 1-57243-696-4

Jumble® Jitterbug
$9.95 • ISBN: 978-1-60078-584-9

Jumble® Jubilee
$9.95 • ISBN: 1-57243-231-4

Jumble® Juggernaut
$9.95 • ISBN: 978-1-60078-026-4

Jumble® Junction
$9.95 • ISBN: 1-57243-380-9

Jumble® Jungle
$9.95 • ISBN: 978-1-57243-961-0

Jumble® Kingdom
$9.95 • ISBN: 1-62937-079-8

Jumble® Knockout
$9.95 • ISBN: 1-62937-078-1

Jumble® Madness
$9.95 • ISBN: 1-892049-24-4

Jumble® Magic
$9.95 • ISBN: 978-1-60078-795-9

Jumble® Marathon
$9.95 • ISBN: 978-1-60078-944-1

Jumble® Safari
$9.95 • ISBN: 978-1-60078-675-4

Jumble® See & Search
$9.95 • ISBN: 1-57243-549-6

Jumble® See & Search 2
$9.95 • ISBN: 1-57243-734-0

Jumble® Sensation
$9.95 • ISBN: 978-1-60078-548-1

Jumble® Surprise
$9.95 • ISBN: 1-57243-320-5

Jumble® University
$9.95 • ISBN: 978-1-62937-001-9

Jumble® Vacation
$9.95 • ISBN: 978-1-60078-796-6

Jumble® Workout
$9.95 • ISBN: 978-1-60078-943-4

Jumpin' Jumble®
$9.95 • ISBN: 978-1-60078-027-1

Lunar Jumble®
$9.95 • ISBN: 978-1-60078-853-6

Outer Space Jumble®
$9.95 • ISBN: 978-1-60078-416-3

Rainy Day Jumble®
$9.95 • ISBN: 978-1-60078-352-4

Ready, Set, Jumble®
$9.95 • ISBN: 978-1-60078-133-0

Rock 'n' Roll Jumble®
$9.95 • ISBN: 978-1-60078-674-7

Royal Jumble®
$9.95 • ISBN: 978-1-60078-738-6

Sports Jumble®
$9.95 • ISBN: 1-57243-113-X

Summer Fun Jumble®
$9.95 • ISBN: 1-57243-114-8

Travel Jumble®
$9.95 • ISBN: 1-57243-198-9

TV Jumble®
$9.95 • ISBN: 1-57243-461-9

Oversize Jumble® Books

More than 500 puzzles each!

Generous Jumble®
$19.95 • ISBN: 1-57243-385-X

Giant Jumble®
$19.95 • ISBN: 1-57243-349-3

Gigantic Jumble®
$19.95 • ISBN: 1-57243-426-0

Jumbo Jumble®
$19.95 • ISBN: 1-57243-314-0

The Very Best of Jumble® BrainBusters
$19.95 • ISBN: 1-57243-845-2

Jumble® Crosswords™

More than 175 puzzles each!

More Jumble® Crosswords™
$9.95 • ISBN: 1-57243-386-8

Jumble® Crosswords™ Jackpot
$9.95 • ISBN: 1-57243-615-8

Jumble® Crosswords™ Jamboree
$9.95 • ISBN: 1-57243-787-1

Jumble® BrainBusters™

More than 175 puzzles each!

Jumble® BrainBusters™
$9.95 • ISBN: 1-892049-28-7

Jumble® BrainBusters™ II
$9.95 • ISBN: 1-57243-424-4

Jumble® BrainBusters™ III
$9.95 • ISBN: 1-57243-463-5

Jumble® BrainBusters™ IV
$9.95 • ISBN: 1-57243-489-9

Jumble® BrainBusters™ 5
$9.95 • ISBN: 1-57243-548-8

Jumble® BrainBusters™ Bonanza
$9.95 • ISBN: 1-57243-616-6

Boggle™ BrainBusters™
$9.95 • ISBN: 1-57243-592-5

Boggle™ BrainBusters™ 2
$9.95 • ISBN: 1-57243-788-X

Jumble® BrainBusters™ Junior
$9.95 • ISBN: 1-892049-29-5

Jumble® BrainBusters™ Junior II
$9.95 • ISBN: 1-57243-425-2

Fun in the Sun with Jumble® BrainBusters™
$9.95 • ISBN: 1-57243-733-2